D1557809

THE ART OF FACT
INVESTIGATION

THE ART OF FACT INVESTIGATION

Creative Thinking in the Age of Information Overload

Philip Segal

Ignaz Press
New York

Published by Ignaz Press
P.O. Box 2897,
Grand Central Station,
New York, NY 10163
Sales@ignazpress.com

Printed in the United States of America.

Cover reproduction courtesy of Philadelphia Museum of Art: A. E. Gallatin Collection, 1952.

ISBN 978-0-9969079-1-0
Library of Congress Control Number 2015916487

For Deborah and Charlie

CONTENTS

Illustrations

Imagination plays an essential role in all human knowledge and we believe that no model of the mind, no matter how esoteric or subtle, can duplicate, much less replace, the imaginative activities of the human mind.

—Peter Tillers and David Schum,
A Theory of Preliminary Fact Investigation

It's not rocket science. Humans are harder than rocket science.

—Edward Tufte

PREFACE

The first thought about writing this book came in Albuquerque the night before I was to give a speech with the title "How to Find Assets Without Breaking the Law" at the invitation of the State Bar of New Mexico's Family Law Institute. A friend who is a family court judge in Albuquerque was going to miss my talk, and her get-to-the-point question involved figuring out how much money someone has: "The thing we always need to know is, what documents should we ask for?"

My answer was that when you have to ask that question too early, you have ceded the high ground. There is no way you can know in all cases and ahead of time what to ask for beyond the general and useless "Everything that's relevant." To know more, you have to *investigate*.

The problem for this experienced, well-respected and overworked judge is the same that millions of other people have each day. Where among the billions of physical and electronic documents do you start looking? Outside of legal cases, there are websites; there is social media; there are public records sitting in courthouse basements, unscanned but sometimes crucially important. Securities records alone on a busy company executive can run to the hundreds or thousands of pages.

As the number of choices of where to look or what to ask for expands, so do the possible avenues of investigation. I have spent a long time trying to explain to people the premise of this book, a concept that is sometimes difficult to grasp if you are not used to working with mounds of information each day: As the amount of information increases, it can be just as time-consuming to find out about people than when the data didn't exist at all. Until you have done a real investigation it is hard to understand what a patchy cloud of suspect data the Internet and databases present to you.

One thing that was on my mind that evening in New Mexico was the idea of representing graphically some of the problems we encounter in gathering and interpreting information. Some people simply understand things better when given an image to consider, but I had yet to devise an image that fit our business. The first rule by graphics authority Edward Tufte is that if you can say something with words more economically than with a picture, forget the picture. For a long while, words seemed better.

Then, looking at a large body of Cubist paintings at the Metropolitan Museum of Art in New York, I found my images. What the Cubists did by breaking "reality" down into elements, considered from a variety of perspectives, is what we do with the hundreds of thousands of bits of information we sort through and collect.

People often tell me, "Your job sounds like fun," and they are right. Fact investigation involves the same kind of educated guessing you need to solve puzzles efficiently. This is the same kind of guessing that Juan Gris, Pablo Picasso and the other Cubists wanted viewers to use in order to figure out what's going on in the paintings they created around 1909 to 1914.

Part of the fun is opening your mind to discovering what you observe. Not what you *expect* you will find, but what you are actually finding. If you like being surprised and having preconceived notions about a person demolished, then you may enjoy investigation. If you are already a busy investigator or litigator and are not forced to blurt out, "I don't believe it!" now and again, you may want to reconsider your methods. There is just too much information out there for any of us to be great predictors of what we will find.

INTRODUCTION

WHY SMALL CHILDREN CAN PLAY MOZART BUT NOT DRAFT WILLS

Investigative lawyers are like other lawyers in that we are problem-solvers, but with one difference. We solve fact investigation problems other lawyers cannot. It is not that we are smarter than other lawyers. What makes us different is that, as in any other part of law or other professions and trades, you get to be good at something by doing a lot of it.

I am sometimes asked what "tricks" or "shortcuts" our office uses to find out things our clients cannot, as if there is some all-problem-solving database that yields the answers people want. There are no tricks to being a good investigator of facts, just as there are no tricks to being a good trial lawyer, doctor or accountant. "Doing" law or medicine is called "practicing," a word that assumes patience and apprenticeship.

One of my law professors once remarked that there are no child-prodigy lawyers. Nobody goes to a seven-year-old to draft a will or analyze a proposed contract. Why should this be, when we see children on the news all the time solving advanced mathematical problems and playing Mozart in concert halls? Part of the answer is that much of the practice of law as well as investigation requires imagination based on life experience.

The ability to appreciate Mozart's harmonies and melodies may be innate in some people. But the thought that, in the Bernard Madoff affair, a business as large as Madoff's should not be audited by a two-man accounting firm in a shopping mall is not an innate notion. Having a suspicion that a tiny auditing firm was too small for such a purportedly large business comes from both learning about how business works and, more importantly, having the imagination to be able to say, "If this were my business and I were honest, how could I possibly run it this way?"

Not only would even a gifted young child have trouble answering this question, but a lot of very expensive "risk management" computer programs failed even to ask it. Questions that are simple in retrospect often need to be asked by human beings with experience, imagination and empathy.

Investigators ask themselves as they work, "What is interesting about a person that is not on his résumé or in newspaper profiles about him? What does he own that is not included in his net worth statement? Even if he has no criminal record, is he associated with organized criminals?" While computers can sort easily through data people enter onto their hard drives, they have a much harder time saying, "Here is something you should expect to find but do not."

Finding answers to these "What's Missing?" questions sounds like a basic skill for a human being, and where lawyers are concerned should certainly be so. But while most lawyers probably spend the bulk of their time outside of a courtroom gathering facts, their time at law school is spent in great part learning about how a small pattern of given facts fits into the part of the law they happen to be studying that semester. Against expectations formed in law school, many lawyers are shocked to find out how much of their livelihood depends on doing the thing for which they received so little training.[1]

INFORMATION SHORTAGE AMID PLENTY

Another surprise awaits those—lawyer and nonlawyer alike—who have ever devoted more than an hour to answering specific questions about a stranger. They are surprised to spend five, 10 or 20 hours and then realize how little information is easily available to them, despite the presence of fast Internet connections and millions of websites boasting extensive public information.

Put your own name into Google. What percentage of what you know about yourself do you find in the results? Everyone you've ever worked for? Every address you've occupied as an adult? A list of your friends and former colleagues? You could keep at it for 24 straight hours, but still come up with 5 percent or less of what there is to know about yourself. And that success rate comes with a big head start because you know search terms about yourself that will help you along. With a stranger, you may know few search terms beyond what the person has chosen to reveal on a résumé.

The fractured digitization of our world means we seemingly have more information available to us, yet it is ever more difficult and time-consuming to track it down. The confident picture that we could once draw about someone has changed to a less clear, Cubist kind of image that forces us to make educated guesses about unclear evidence. We need to choose from the many perspectives available to us how to evaluate each fact a computer hands us.

The man who 30 years ago would have spent most of his life in a single town, working at a single company, spending time with the same group of friends, has become a lot more difficult to profile. Chances are that he has moved around more than he would have a generation ago. And even if he hasn't moved much, the information about him has. It could now be almost anywhere.

Consider the following two problems. To see how an investigator would have solved them, read the rest of this book or turn immediately to Appendix I, where a short description can be found on each of these real-life cases.

PROBLEM 1—ORGANIZED CRIMINAL OR REGULAR BUSINESSMAN?

The general counsel at a Fortune 100 company has been asked to evaluate a prospective business partner on rumors that he is linked to organized crime.

She is told that the prospective partner has no criminal record, but her company needs to conduct a discreet asset search to see if there were companies or associates in the prospective partner's past that he has not disclosed and that could come back to harm the company's reputation later on. Any side companies the prospective partner may have could be incorporated in a number of U.S. states and perhaps even overseas.

An avid reader of Sherlock Holmes mysteries, the general counsel remembers the advice Holmes gave in *A Study in Scarlet:* "It is a capital mistake to theorize before you have all the evidence. It biases the judgment."

One of her assistants asks her, "How can we know when we'll have all the evidence?" Another offers that well-hidden companies are just that—well hidden. "How do we know when to stop looking? How do we know where to start?" If the prospective partner owned a bunch of apartment buildings in the name of Exelone Properties of Arizona or Amalgamated St. Pete Real Estate of Florida, how would the general counsel's legal team be able to figure this out?

Beyond checking criminal records and without coming right out and asking the man's friends whether he is involved in organized crime, where among the millions of facts and places to look should the team begin its task?

PROBLEM 2—MILLIONS OF EMAILS, TWO WEEKS TO FIND IT

A prominent litigator is involved in a billion-dollar lawsuit and is looking at spending the next two years in discovery, the delicate dance that occurs before big cases go to trial. He has asked his opponents to produce documents relevant to the case, but their counsel produced little of value and claimed the request was "overly broad." The other side, a gigantic bank with thousands of branches all over the world and an opaque, complicated administrative structure, claims to have no idea what our litigator wants.

He needs computer records about a particular line of business at the bank, but has no idea who at the bank compiles computer records, which department this person belongs to or even which of the bank's eight computer systems he needs to ask about. Worse still, different branches used different systems, depending on how old the systems were and whether the branches had been acquired from other banks or were originally part of the defendant bank.

Our litigator's judge is not allowing him to ask for "all relevant investment banking" documents, but when he asked for documents from the investment or merchant banking departments, he found that the ones he wanted were not included. It turned out those were produced by a department that, following a corporate reorganization, had been renamed and reported to a different division. He needed the name of the department and division. With hundreds of millions of emails in the company's servers, he couldn't ask for all of them but needed to name emails of employees whose names he didn't know.

Time was running out and litigation costs were mounting fast.

While this book has advice about where to look for information (and where not to look if you are interested in obeying the law), it starts off in Chapter 1 on how to realize what it is you are looking at. That will make it easier to absorb the message of Chapter 2, which is that since you can't look at every document and interview everyone, good investigation requires guesswork. The remainder of the book contains information about the sources of information we use, and finally the way we stay on the right side of the law and the rules of professional ethics and some tips on how to speak to people when, as it often does, computer-based searching fails to deliver all the information we need.

—1—

Farewell Sherlock Holmes, Hello Picasso

We are told every day that we live in an age in which we are overloaded with information. Usually it is not all the information we need.

Life today is no longer (if it ever was) like a Sherlock Holmes story. There, an investigator gets the "answer" based on evidence in a confined space from one of a handful of people in close physical proximity. This evidence is staring the investigator—and everyone else not as brilliant—right in the face. "Eliminate all other factors, and the one which remains must be the truth," Holmes said. [2] We will see in the next chapter that Holmes reached his conclusions not through logical deductions but by making a lot of educated guesses. That is the way investigators always have to operate.

The Holmes stories worked on the charming notion that all evidence is sitting there in the open, waiting for a sharp-eyed person to look at it and put it together into a coherent story. Nobody could do such a thing today. People, things, information (including money in its electronic form) could be—literally—anywhere on earth. The first step toward becoming better at investigation is to recognize this. Thinking about the process you use to track down information is as important as evaluating the information when you find it.

THE VIEWER AS DETECTIVE

Think of the old way of investigation as looking at a traditional Western, post-Renaissance portrait. Much of the information is right in front of the viewer, just the way a background investigation might have worked in the 1950s on a person who had lived his entire life in a single neighborhood. For the portrait viewer, it was about looking at the visual information. This was subject to the artist's interpretation, but the information was immediately recognizable. Use of perspective made the background realistic. The subject was lit in a way that made sense based on the sources of light in the picture. There were emotional subtleties that varied with each face, perhaps a reference to be researched in the title of a book the subject was holding. But profound, head-scratching mystery was rare.

For most legal investigations in the age of the traditional portrait, everyone who knew anything about most of the subjects would be living in a small geographic area. All of a person's work colleagues, his relatives, friends, all of his assets—would usually be easy to get at. Records of what he had said to casual acquaintances 25 years before would be in a diary if you could find it, or in someone's pile of saved letters. Otherwise, those remarks would be lost forever.

Then, decades before computers and the Internet radically transformed the way we look at fact gathering, there was an equally dramatic transformation in the way visual artists conveyed information. The idea originated by the Cubist painters of the early 20th century was that viewers of art needed to be investigators. The skills Cubists sought to encourage in their viewers are the same ones fact investigators need to use today.

In systematically dismantling naturalistic representation, the Cubists were inspired by the writing of Sigmund Freud, who believed that conscious and unconscious thinking were both at work all the time. As a result, art historians Ernst Kris and Ernst Gombrich came to believe that "because the visible world we experience is constructed in part from what we perceive and part from our memories of sights, smells movements and touch," that "the act of viewing is an elaborate and creative mental process."[3]

The beholder's involvement—the viewer's exercise or struggle to figure out what he is looking at—was as important to the Cubists as the object itself. For lawyers today, drowning in millions of pages of potential evidence and with millions of places to look for information on the Internet, how we search for and sort through information merits the same kind of attention.

The viewer as detective was especially pertinent in the work of Juan Gris (1887-1927). Gris was a big fan of the original pulp fiction—installment stories in France of the "elusive, brilliant criminal figure Fantômas, a man whose face nobody ever saw and who remained uncatchable by the police."[4] Fantômas figures in one of the greatest paintings by Gris, *The Man at the Café* from 1914 (Figure 1).

As in many Cubist works, it is not the abundance of information that is alluring in this painting but the absence of it: "Criminality hovers here like the shadow cast against the back wall."[5] The only way to see the size of the hat is to look at the shadow it casts because the actual object itself is mostly hidden. We have complete confidence from this painting that when he's finished his paper and his beer, Fantômas will get up and walk out, still a free man.

I think of shadows all the time when we are assigned to search for assets (more on this in Chapters 2 and 4). Like the face and hat in *The Man at the Café,* cash in the bank account of a stranger is nearly impossible to see. But cash casts shadows in objects purchased, in companies controlled and in debts registered. Find the things that reflect the cash and you will have a good idea of where the cash came from and how much may be left.

MULTIPLE PERSPECTIVES

The Cubists anticipated another difficulty of fact investigation— multiple perspectives. The artists reasoned that if our conscious and unconscious minds are always both on duty interpreting what we see, there is more than one perspective from which to consider anything. There is no rule about which perspective gets us to the truth, because often we need to sort, balance and then blend the conclusions from different perspectives to get to our best guess about what the truth may be.

In another wonderful Cubist classic, Picasso's 1909 *Carafe and Candlestick* (Fig. 2) the carafe is below us, the stem of the glass is seen straight on and the candlestick is slightly above us. All of this on the same presumably flat table, while the viewer doesn't move an inch. The sense of confusion about what we are looking at is something that fact investigators face all the time.

Juan Gris, *The Man at the Café*, 1914

Pablo Picasso, *Carafe and Candlestick*, 1909

Georges Braque, *Trees at L'Estaque*, 1908

René Magritte, *The Eternally Obvious (L'Évidence éternelle),* 1930

Joseph Jastrow, Duck-Rabbit Illusion, 1899

Copyright © Scott Adams, Inc., 2010

We find a court document on the Internet about a person's legal battles with a former partner. We read the document and see that this case is part of a larger series of cases that involve the two partners and other people as well. Where does this case stand in the series? Near the end, or is it the one that set off the chain of fights? We are not even sure whether this is an important fight worth our time and budget to unravel.

Should we be "above" the case (taking it in from 40,000 feet as in a jet plane) or should we get down to ground level and dissect its details for what they can reveal about our man? Picasso had no "right" answer about which view of the objects was "correct," because his point was that it depended on something outside the picture—the viewer. In an investigation, we need to take educated guesses about which way to view a legal or factual issue. The perspective we need to keep in mind is our client's. That perspective, for the purposes of *this investigation only,* is the correct one.

Sometimes time and money prevent us from finishing an investigation—from searching for and possibly retrieving all the documents we think we need. Documents go missing from archives or take months to be located. We are able to retrieve some cases, but the documents tell us only that the matter was settled. Perhaps we can learn about the terms of the settlement only from interviewing people involved in the matter. If they decline to speak to us (or are dead or unfindable), then what? Then we have an investigation like *Carafe and Candlestick:* We are not entirely sure how to interpret what we are looking at. We have to admit that what we have does not make complete sense.

The confusion can be even more basic than one of perspective. Look again at *Carafe and Candlestick.* Picasso makes it impossible to know for certain how many pears there are in this picture. When we look for "Joseph L. Taylor" in supposedly all-knowing (but really error-filled) databases, we can come across many listings for someone with the same name and address. Which one pertains to "our" man? In some databases the men will have different Social Security numbers. In others, the numbers will be the same. Some databases differentiate between Joseph Sr.

and Joseph Jr., while some will refer to the second man as Joseph II. Later we may find a newspaper article that mentions Joseph L. Taylor at that address, a widower with no children.

Are there two Joseph Taylors after all, with a misinformed newspaper reporter? Or is there just one Taylor with a lot of data errors that require sorting through? There was no right answer about the number of pears, but given enough time we may be able to sort out the right number of Joseph Taylors. (We go into detail on the question of databases in Chapter 4.)

Maybe we can sort out the Taylor problem at our computers, but maybe not. The modern reality is that just as we can stare forever at Picasso's work and not know the number of pears there are, we can look all we want at databases and public records, but we may need to move on to interviewing relatives and neighbors or Mr. Taylor himself (see Chapter 6). Of course, while there is no interview to be done about the number of pears Picasso portrayed, and while we can talk to friends and neighbors about the Taylor family, there are plenty of investigations in which budget constraints forbid interviews, or clients rule them out for fear that the investigation will show itself. Like the number of pears in the picture, the number of Joseph Taylors could remain a mystery.

Depersonalization to Get to the Truth

The Cubists often largely did away with the kind of perspective people had become used to seeing in paintings. In a picture without depth, it is up to the viewer to make associations to figure out what he is seeing. This was willful depersonalization. The Cubists thought that in meditating on the elements of the truth, a perceived form broken up into geometric parts was closer to pure reality than reproducing the scene in a conventionally "realistic" way.

In *Trees at L'Estaque* by Georges Braque (1882-1963) (Fig. 3) the landscape "does not seem to have any space for human habitation—a feeling that is reinforced by the windowless houses and by the way the road running between the two trees is so immaterial that one can hardly imagine a human foot being placed on it."[6]

Depersonalization would seem to be the enemy of an investigator who seeks to paint a full picture of a candidate for a board position or a key witness in a court case. How can depersonalization become a way into seeing truth, when we are looking at expanding what we know about a person?

Depersonalization is part of the methodology of investigation, not the end in itself. We need to break up a person's life so that we can see what is missing in our picture before putting together the truest representation of that life that we can. (Cubist Juan Gris once said that he "began with an abstraction in order to arrive at a true fact."[7]) Just because a picture or an investigation breaks a landscape or a person's life into its component parts does not mean the components have no relationship with one another. It is the reverse. In breaking the parts up it is easier to see how they work together.

As schoolchildren we all learn that simply memorizing dates of events is very dull and is knowledge soon forgotten. History comes alive when an event on a particular date is explained by what caused it to happen, what the event may have felt like at the time and what it set off in the future. In other words, history is more interesting when it is told as a story.

Each person's life is a story too, but we need to break up the facts presented to us in order to arrange them into something that will make chronological sense. There will be many gaps in the story, but arranging a person's life chronologically exposes those gaps and allows us to ask about them further or to note that we have a less than full sense of a person.

We will see later in Chapter 3 the importance of chronologies to sort out disparate elements of a person's life, but chronologies are not enough. In looking at pieces of a life, investigators verify them, uncover previously unknown facts and then connect them to things that are happening to—or around—the person. These are things which may not have made it into the authorized biography or soft magazine feature, but they may still have influenced the life we are examining. We need to put all events (the date of graduation, the day the war started, the day the company was sued for a fraud) in chronological order to make some sense of them.

The blending of categories of information (personal, business, social, historical) is not intuitive to some. We look not just at what a person wants us to know about him (a résumé or official biography), nor just what others have to say about him. Both are relevant because the unreal parts of a background investigation contribute to a more full view of a person.

What people aspire to is part of the reality of who they are, if not what they do. Even if a subject invents a job that never existed or pretends to be from a higher economic class than he really is, a client may decide nonetheless to go ahead and be his partner in business because this man has unusual access to a particular market or industry. It is for the better to know his vulnerabilities and tendencies before signing up to a long business relationship.

The urge to categorize information is something Picasso fought with his painted *Guitar* sculptures in 1913 and 1914. These confused and upset viewers who wondered whether they were looking at sculptures or paintings. Picasso was having fun in blurring the lines between the two mediums—lines that do nothing to help us arrive at the "truth" of a guitar, which in reality is multicolored and three-dimensional. Searchers for reality may be getting short-changed by considering only paintings that are two-dimensional or three-dimensional figures that are not painted.

Rejecting Paint by Number Investigation

Relying on profiles of people in the newspaper or on websites that those people control is like painting by numbers. You can alter colors, but the forms and relationships between those forms remain unchangeable. If over 25 years it has been written dozens of times that a person graduated from the Stanford Graduate School of Business, it would take a brazen reporter to say to the celebrity who has consented to an interview, "You say you went to Stanford—prove it." So, after a while journalists and sloppy investigators paint by numbers and, based on no good evidence, assume that the Stanford degree is genuine.[8]

Only by starting from the ground up and verifying what "everyone knows" to be true, (that he went to Stanford) do we find that he left school three credits short of a degree. Only by finding out that the business someone started after college then went bankrupt in late 1998 can we put into proper perspective a quote in a newspaper profile that "I had decided that business was too stressful and spent 1999 in Asia to find myself."

For the Cubists, all superficial information was up for reconsideration, and so should it be with the open-minded investigator. Less than 20 years after the Cubists came a different but equally modern take on information by René Magritte (1898-1967), an artist who was fascinated and disturbed by what mechanization and photography were doing to painting.

L'Évidence éternelle (The Eternally Obvious) (Fig. 4) was a radical—some have called it violent—work that emphasizes how much the camera has changed the way we see things. Of this painting, critic John Berger wrote that any of the parts can be removed or they can be arranged in a different order. "What appears to exist … may be seen as a series of discontinuous movable parts."[9]

The more information there is to get about a person, the more it can feel like this Magritte painting, but chopped up into hundreds of parts that individually are not so obviously fitted into a whole that makes sense. When we investigate a complicated life, the order in which we find the disparate elements is so unpredictable that two separate investigations that retrieve all the same information could turn up that information in different, unrecognizable orders.

If you need court records from two counties in Massachusetts, three counties in Texas and two in California, you cannot know for certain in which order the results will get to you. If you are searching even on Google (more on this in Chapter 3), results vary by time of day, the location from which the search is being done and, of course, word order used in the search. The same word order can turn up different results hours apart. Search strings in identical databases will turn up different lists of news articles, and so on. It is the way we reorder the jumble of results that should matter more than the order in which the results come to us.

What the camera did to painting (at least for Magritte), computers and jet travel have done to information gathering. If we can get anywhere on Earth in 24 hours, the information about us can get there many times faster. Instead of a concise portrait of a person's life, the best we can often hope for is a Magritte-like portrait with spaces replacing the missing parts. The body parts will sometimes be mixed up, but we hope there will be enough of them to figure out a rough, proper order.

Archaeology of the Here and Now

Rather than painting a portrait of a person, the activity of observing and sorting through information often makes me think of myself as an archaeologist for the world of last month or last year. We are digging for material buried not as deeply as shards of clay in eastern Anatolia, but still scattered over a very wide area—in some cases the entire world.

Archaeologists seldom get the kind of validation of their theories that investigators do. Nobody will come forward and say, "You're right. Despite what is written about our ancient civilization, we were planting three crops a year much earlier on than what scientists in the 19th century used to think."

Investigators can come a lot closer to the "You're right" moment. Real life is exciting, as both investigators and archaeologists can appreciate. What happens in real life is abstracted by signals, increasingly irregular the more remote the past events. Archaeologists and investigators are then faced with the same job: to assemble a jumble of facts into a coherent story that will try to explain what happened and why. All investigators—archaeologists included—are in the business of turning signals back into a semblance of real life.

Where to begin looking for the assets of a person that could be hidden anywhere? Archaeologists approaching a new site on which to dig do not deploy any kind of rigid rule about where to begin. It will depend on the terrain, what they already know about the area, whether there are any structures left standing and other factors. Wherever they begin, they will of course keep careful records of where they've already looked.

Investigators with an open mind work in a similar way. There is no unbreakable rule about which part of the public record we need to search first to find out about a person. We will want to look at the entire "field" of a person's life if we can, but would probably not start with securities records when we know that Mr. Johnson ran a chain of dry cleaners that never went public. Securities records could reveal something interesting about a part of his life he's kept hidden until now, but they may not be the most important place to look.

Like archaeologists, investigators assemble what appear to be unconnected facts into a comprehensible story. Mr. Johnson has (or had) a thriving business. What happened to it? How did it do? Unless you can ask him or his associates—not always feasible—you need to look at the modern day equivalent of pottery and old tools: legal and financial records.

ACCOUNTING, ABSTRACTION, RECONSTITUTION

When the Cubists had broken down the elements of what they saw to an extent that bordered on abstraction, they stopped and turned back. In 1911 they started inserting clues into their paintings—strips of newsprint, puns and other tips—so that viewers would have a firmer notion of what was in the artist's mind when the picture was made.

Accounting is language that gives you an abstracted but still intelligible look at both a series of events over the course of a year and a moment frozen in time (the financial year-end). As difficult as it may be for the uninitiated to read a financial report, a little bit of training in the terminology of accounting reveals that it is a dialect of the language you speak for people who don't like to talk and are not big on detail. You have to learn the dialect, and then do some guessing at what those words mean.

We might say to ourselves and then brief a client this way: "Johnson's dry-cleaning chain had two good years in a row, but around the end of year two, business began to slip when he hired some dreadful people who tended to open the shops late and close early, and year three was bad when Johnson changed his chemical supplier and quality suffered." We would get this from the language of accounting, which could report

> Net profit in year one was 82 percent above the profit of the year before, while in year two the earnings were up 72 percent. However the earnings in year one were reliant on asset sales for just 5 percent of the total earnings whereas in year two asset sales comprised three-quarters of the earnings. Net profit in year three was down 21 percent compared with year two, amid impairment charges and restated earnings from year two to reflect increased professional fees.

Only by moving from the statistics to the cases against the bad employees and interviews with other former workers and suppliers could we slowly begin to assemble a fairly good picture of what happened to Johnson's business.

The legal records surrounding Johnson's business and the records of his asset sales are not just lying around in the open. Sherlock Holmes frequently remarks to Watson that "he sees just what everyone else sees, only he has trained himself to apply his method in order to determine the full significance of his perceptions."[10] Nothing could be more different from the world that presents itself to the modern investigator. Information is buried in remote courthouse basements, tucked away on obscure websites, mentioned in passing in newspaper stories that are hard to retrieve because the keyword has a typographical error. Key witnesses can be hard to find and harder to persuade to talk.

Investigators need to rely on inference in deciphering information and even in deciding where to look for it, but what kind of inference is best? That is the subject of the next chapter. It won't sound satisfactory to those who want the certitude of a solid portrait of Henry VIII or the neat and tidy solutions of many a detective novel. It is something we need to recognize is going to be part of any good investigation: imagination and guesswork.

—2—

WHY AN OPEN MIND GETS BETTER RESULTS: GUESSWORK IN THE AGE OF INFORMATION OVERLOAD

"Fact investigation" and "imagination" strike many as mutually exclusive terms. Investigation is usually thought to be about observing, digging up more things to examine, sorting it all out and presenting it as a story that is easy to understand.

In the last chapter we saw that active observation and deciphering clues are part of any investigation. But isn't imagination used to invent things and concepts? Most people would define investigation as sorting through what we can find that already exists—not the invention of anything.

Invented things are never wholly new. They are new combinations of existing compounds; new arrangements of musical notes already known. New novels that captivate us can be said to be reinventing plots well known through the ages. But even if you define imagination this way, other than the fitting of facts into a new theory of law, some still struggle to understand why a lawyer would need to imagine or invent anything when collating a bunch of facts.

The truth is that investigators use imagination all the time for the simple reason that you can't search everywhere and look at everything. Detective stories featuring all the suspects in one room of a country mansion are entertaining, but real-life investigation is infinitely more complex.

Imagining the order of Magritte's *L'Évidence éternelle*, a "puzzle" of just five pieces, is an extreme case on the easy end of the scale, but it was still radical in its day and still speaks to our problem with information today.

Given a jigsaw puzzle with 20 pieces, you could methodically try to fit each piece with every other piece until you had the thing solved. At one second per attempt, this would take you a maximum of about 44 minutes (20 seconds times 19, 19 times 18, 18 times 17, etc.). With five million pieces, you would still be at it at the end of your life. The only way to get through that large a puzzle is to imagine that this tiny bit of blue is less likely to be a face than part of the sky. You would make such decisions hundreds and hundreds of times. The smaller, 20-piece puzzle would never take as long as 44 minutes because the fewer the pieces, the more evident the reasoning shortcuts.

Investigation is about making bets about the best way forward. Making bets means figuring probabilities, which requires imagining the future. Investigators not only analyze the evidence that's in front of them. They also must *move toward and uncover the evidence* before they can begin trying to make sense of it. Where in the world do you start when the evidence could be anywhere? Some decisions are easy. If a person appears never to have left the United States, your first step will not be to search public records in Argentina or Nigeria. But even with "only" the United States or even just California to search, shortcuts are essential.

TRILLIONS OF POSSIBILITIES, 24 HOURS TO FIND AN ANSWER

A one-in-a-trillion problem was what British codebreakers during the Second World War woke up to each day, faced with the task of breaking the codes set by Nazi Germany's famed Enigma encryption machine. Every day, the British would intercept coded German messages, knowing they would have no more than 24 hours to break the code because Enigma would use one of trillions of new encryption combinations every day.

The Enigma team in Britain was portrayed in the movie "The Imitation Game." The film shows that the breakthrough by team leader Alan Turing came in part because of a machine that plodded through millions of possibilities, as in the jigsaw example above. But through most of the movie, the machine is defeated by the sheer number of combinations it must try and the limited amount of time it has to solve the problem.

As in the jigsaw example, code breakers take shortcuts. They use the frequency of letters and repeated words to predict likelihoods that certain combinations are right and others are wrong. If the most common letter in German is e, then the chance is better than average that the most common letter in a bunch of coded messages stands for e.

Unfortunately, this kind of elementary educated guessing didn't get Turing's team very far because encoders knew that code breakers would be looking at just these features. The trillions of possible enigma codes and the tiny one-day sample of codes to work with proved too much for Turing's team and their machine. The breakthrough came when team members put themselves in the shoes of the people they were fighting. The team realized that the phrase "Heil Hitler!" probably appeared at the end of each message the Germans sent. It was a fatal flaw that helped to break Enigma (without letting the Germans know, of course) and turn the tide of World War II.

Turing and his team could never be 100 percent certain that the messages ended in "Heil Hitler," but it was a sensible bet. Sensible, because they used information they had from open propaganda, articles meant for wide dispersal, and they *imagined* (i.e. assumed without proof) that the pattern they had seen could have been be repeated in secret code. Of course, it was a tremendous blunder to place a consistent phrase in a consistent spot in one coded message after another. But the other bit of imagination that served Turing well was that he recognized the Enigma system and Germany's messaging for what they were—the product of fallible human beings. (In Chapter 4, we will examine the illogical, jumbled mess of databases, and how dealing with them is not unlike dealing with eccentric people.)

THE CONTEXT OF DISCOVERY AND BANK ACCOUNTS

The kind of imagination that investigators use when they try to form an explanatory hypothesis for something they observe is called abductive reasoning, in which conclusions *may*—but need not always—follow from a premise.

The credit for identifying and naming the process of abduction goes to an American philosopher, Charles Sanders Peirce (1839-1914). What is most striking about this is that abduction appears to have been largely overlooked and under-analyzed by almost 2,400 years of formal logic and philosophy.[11]

As Peirce wrote, abduction "is the only logical operation which introduces any new idea."[12] While "Deduction proves that something *must* be .... Abduction merely suggests that something *may be*."[13] Novices to investigation may ask: How could we prefer finding that something *may* be to finding that something *must* be? In short, because life usually does not present us with enough known facts early on to deduce anything.

The classic example to illustrate abduction is well known in philosophy circles. Normal deduction would present us with a rule such as "All the beans from this bag are white." Then we would be presented with a "case" that says, "These beans are from this bag." Logically, our result would be, "These beans are white." There is no other conclusion possible as to the color of the beans.

But what if we didn't know where the beans came from? No logical deduction would be possible. Instead, we would start with the same rule that all beans from this bag are white. Then we would observe that these beans are white, but the idea that the beans are from the bag must just be a theory. Not all white beans in the world need to have come from this bag, after all.

If we can establish independently that the beans come from the bag, then the neat-looking deduction above can be rolled out. Otherwise, we are left with something less than airtight.

Now instead of beans in a bag, think about money in a bank account controlled by Mr. Jackson.

We may know that all the money in a particular account is Jackson's, and we suspect the money we have seen directed to a bad company came from this account. Therefore Jackson probably funds the bad company. Nice and neat if you can prove it, but how do you know the money is from this account if you can't look at the account? In the United States, the inner functioning of a bank account is the hardest thing to find if you don't wish to break the law or get a court order. (See Chapter 5 on investigating without breaking the law.)

The best you can do is to say: "All the money in a particular account is Jackson's. We don't know exactly where the bad company's funding is coming from, but we observe that all the same people in Jackson's other ventures we have discovered are associated with this company at the same address. Therefore the idea that Jackson is funding the company is just a theory (but perhaps a good one)."

We still don't have proof. Jackson could have arranged outside funders for the company. Jackson could also be a front man with no equity interest in the company. As with the beans, we will need independent verification that the company was funded by Jackson. Court documents from litigation involving the company could help, as could interviews with people who sued the company or worked there.

Even all of this will not be proof to satisfy a logician, and it may not even be proof beyond a reasonable doubt. But it could be persuasive enough in a civil case (which usually requires a more-likely-than-not standard of probability). It could also help negotiations with Jackson to speed matters up toward a satisfactory conclusion by settlement.

This kind of abductive discovery is really what is going on nearly all the time during an investigation—even the fictitious kind. In *The Sign of The Four*, Sherlock Holmes "deduces" that Watson has been to the post office to send a telegram, based on two observations: that Watson had some red-tinted earth on his shoe (of a kind found only in the neighborhood opposite the post office) and that Watson already had plenty of letters and stamps in his desk.

Holmes therefore figures that Watson had gone out to send a telegram from the post office, and of course—because it's a novel about how smart Holmes is—that turns out to be correct. This is abduction (guessing) dressed up as deduction. Watson could have walked by the post office without going in. He might have gone inside the post office to meet a friend, pick up a package or buy more stamps of different denominations. There was nothing that proved the theory that he had been to the post office to send a telegram.[14]

Holmes guessed (and therefore theorized) all the time while asserting that he was just making logical deductions based on observations. His claimed refusal to embrace any hypothesis until "all" evidence is available is a luxury that we can seldom afford. Investigations of any complexity always operate on hypotheses, subject to frequent revision.

Case Study: The Phony Bankruptcy and the Sham Divorce

A recently divorced man who owed our client more than $1 million immediately went bankrupt when his divorce became final. We assumed initially that his ex-wife must have received a great deal of money if the settlement drove him into bankruptcy. Then we looked at the divorce settlement that happened to be in a state that makes these public, and our opinion changed.

The entire two-year battle in court was over the custody of a child who did not have special needs and who was about to turn 18. There was not a word in the settlement about dividing up money. Nothing illegal or illogical here, but this struck us, and would strike most people, as very odd.

Our client had not even known whether his debtor was married. It turned out that the debtor's ex-wife of just a few months had a very prosperous business formed during the marriage. They lived in a state that equitably divided marital property, and there was no prenuptial agreement on the record. Based on these facts, the husband would have had a claim for roughly half the business. The long court battle over custody without a word about millions of dollars looked even more unlikely.

We then found that the spouses had been buying real property in their own names for years. If they had been living apart for such a long period, we would have expected a fight over the money, unless they wanted information about the valuable business to remain private. When we then found that the husband had continued working at his wife's business right up until the divorce, we developed a thesis:

We suspected that the husband was still working at the company and had lied to the bankruptcy court by suppressing the fact that he had a share in the business. This made creditors such as our client less willing to spend money to go after the husband to try to collect the husband's debts.

A short time later, we were able to prove that the husband worked at the wife's business both before and after the divorce. We still had no logical proof that he was a co-owner of the business, but the circumstantial evidence was good enough for our client to keep up the pressure on the debtor in order to extract a favorable settlement.

You can see in the case study that we never would have found the divorce if we had not decided at the outset to comb the public record for everything we could find about this man. As we will see in Chapter 3, beginning with the public record is nearly always a must because clients know less than they think about the people they want us to investigate.

Abduction is closely related to another type of reasoning that Peirce called "retroduction."[15] Briefly put, thinking abductively invents possibilities that would explain otherwise inexplicable evidence. Imagine a man named Foster had $20 million six months ago, but now he says he is broke. We abduce that Foster had a bad year, that Foster was lying when he said he had $20 million, or that Foster was truthful about his $20 million before but is lying now.

Retroduction reverses this and imagines evidence that one of these possibilities could generate. For instance, if he is lying now we might see that he fraudulently sold his main asset to his wife to evade creditors. We would look for a deed transfer for his home or evidence that his business changed ownership.

In the case of Foster, we should be open to the possibility of evidence to support or refute any of the three possibilities (bad year, lying then, lying now) as well as evidence that would lead us to a fourth conclusion not yet imagined (e.g. he had just $5.8 million six months ago and is down to $1.2 million now—not enough to pay all of his debts but not broke either).

Abduction's Risks

We do not need a lot of certainty for something to be entered into evidence. Rule 401 of the U.S. Federal Rules of Evidence says evidence is relevant if it has *any* tendency to make a fact more or less probable than it would be without the evidence. In civil matters, a jury only has to find that an allegation of liability is "more likely true than not true," which is how juries are typically instructed. Even in a criminal case in which guilt needs to be demonstrated "beyond a reasonable doubt" this can never mean 100 percent certainty, because "there are very few things in this world that we know with absolute certainty." [16]

This is worth keeping in mind when an investigator (or anyone else) tries to tell you he has "proof" of some fact or theory. His evidence may be persuasive without being ironclad, and that leaves us in the realm of abduction, not cold, hard logic.

But even though you can get evidence admitted when it moves the needle only a little bit, better evidence is always going to be preferable to weaker evidence. The question for anyone using an investigator is, when do you decide that you've got the strongest evidence you're going to get?

Suppose you are asked to profile a person who has lived and worked in 15 different jurisdictions over the past 20 years. If you cannot afford the time and money to search courthouses for litigation in all of these, you need a hypothesis about the ones most likely to yield information. So you search in the five that account for 12 of the person's 15 residences and workplaces in the past 20 years. If he was arrested for assault while on vacation or in a county adjacent to the one in which he worked, you may miss it. If you happen to learn about a vacation arrest late in the investigation through an interview, you need to go to a courthouse that was not on your original list. If you find out that your man changed his name 10 years ago, you need to go back and search again under his older name.

What happens if you decide that your budget doesn't support even that much searching? Leaving out three residences from 15 sounds like a lot, but if you argue that you searched 80 percent of a person's residential jurisdictions, that sounds more thorough. Whatever your decision about where to look, there is no "proof" of a clean record if you find nothing. There is only a very thorough (or perhaps just reasonably conducted) search that yielded no results.

The extreme kind of abduction is when we need to have not one hypothesis but a series of assumptions—none of which we can prove for the moment—in order to get to an entire hypothesis that can be tested. If the hypothesis turns out to be true, most or all of the assumptions will turn out to be right as well, but we have to make the leap of faith before we find out. This is what Umberto Eco calls "meta-abduction."[17]

CASE STUDY: META-ABDUCTION AND THE MYSTERIOUS PURCHASING AGENT

We were looking over thousands of emails in the discovery phase of an after-fraud investigation, seeking evidence that a group of three employees had ripped off the business owner. One suspicious piece of evidence was the high price the company was paying for a certain kind of equipment that the company bought hundreds of units of each year. Instead of buying the equipment directly from the manufacturer 20 miles away, the employees under suspicion used a purchasing agent in Chicago, a thousand miles away. The only identifying information for the agent was a Chicago cellphone number (a throwaway phone we could not trace to an owner) and a Gmail account.

The name of the Chicago agent was William Smith, and there were dozens of William Smiths who could have been our man. We spent weeks trying to figure out who he was. Then, something occurred to us: There were plenty of emails between our people and William Smith regarding the ordering of the equipment. But in the dozens of emails between Smith's colleagues on the subject of this equipment, they never once discussed Smith or even referred to him in passing. This was a man who was responsible for selling them several hundred thousand dollars a year of equipment, yet all discussion about the procurement of the equipment referred to an employee called Peewee, as in, "Make sure Peewee gets the new shipment [of equipment] in by the 28th." We never knew who Peewee was, and would have liked to be able to ask him about Smith. Then, weeks later, the aunt of one of the fraudsters (two of whom were brothers) wrote to the elder one inviting him and his brother for Thanksgiving dinner. Since she used the elder brother's work email, it had been produced in discovery. In her email, the aunt made it clear that the younger brother (whose name we knew to be Ernest), went by Peewee as a family nickname. Finally, we noticed that nobody ever seemed to email Peewee about the equipment.

Our new theory was that that William Smith and Peewee were the same person. That is, William Smith was an invented middleman whose markup on the equipment was being pocketed by the brothers.

In our meta-abduction in the case study above, how many assumptions did we need to make?

1. The price for the equipment was unreasonably high.

2. The use of a purchasing agent was suspicious.

3. A purchasing agent with no fixed address and a Gmail account was odd.

4. It was also odd that we saw no internal discussion about—but plenty of email correspondence with—someone selling the company so much equipment.

5. Just as odd, and in complete contrast to No. 4, we saw a lot of internal discussion about a fellow employee involved with the same transactions but no correspondence with him.

None of this was proof that would allow a logical deduction, but it was certainly persuasive enough for our clients to become much more aggressive in questioning the other side about the equipment purchase. However, in other cases some of our assumptions could have turned out to be wrong, and the whole theory would have collapsed.

Another risk that comes with abduction is that it leaves open the possibility that you can be wrong by getting carried away with the "fallacy of the converse," also known as *post hoc ergo propter hoc*. This is the mistake of confusing two facts with cause and effect.

We see a net worth statement that says Carson is worth $9 million and that he lives on a large Montana ranch. Does this mean that Carson owns the ranch? Not necessarily, but we would certainly spend time looking into the ownership of the company that owns the ranch, on the theory that it may be owned by Carson.

If we had found that Carson had declared bankruptcy twice in the past three years, had defaulted on a ton of debts and had allowed his mother to be evicted from her home after she defaulted on her mortgage, then we would still look at the ownership of the ranch. Carson may have hidden his ownership from the bankruptcy court or acquired the ranch after bankruptcy. Without knowledge of the ownership of the ranch, we cannot know whether Carson is rich and heartless with regard to his mother, or genuinely impoverished.

Only after establishing who owns the ranch can our picture of Carson's relationship to the land and the holding company be laid out in an irrefutably logical sentence.

Why Big Data Is No Solution

A third kind of reasoning most often associated with the scientific method is called induction. Induction is a way of thinking that allows us to infer a rule based on many observations. But like abduction, it does not offer deductive proof. We might say of Jackson above, "Since we have often observed in the past that a person's companies are funded by him, if we find companies owned by Jackson it's likely he funded those too."

Both abduction and induction are ampliative, which means that their conclusions go beyond what is (logically) contained in their premises. The difference is that in abduction there is an appeal to explanatory considerations, but in induction there is an appeal only to observed frequencies or statistics.[18]

I am asked sometimes how much the rise of computers using "big data" helps in doing an investigation. Many people are surprised when I treat big data as largely irrelevant to the high-end fact investigation. Big data is computerized induction, the idea that we can *in aggregate* predict all kinds of relationships between people, places and things.[19] It is useful for figuring out where the next outbreak of a disease may strike, but in aggregate is the opposite of what the investigation of a particular person, company or situation demands: disaggregation into small component parts.

Big data is happy to chuck causation over the side of the ship in favor of correlation, whereas we want both: correlation of elements in a life that may help us with causation. So much of what investigators want to find out involves human states of mind, while big data has no time for individual states of mind: Who cares about one individual decision when we can talk in general about millions?

In our investigations we often see that a person we are looking at is associated with several companies and several addresses, all at the same time but in locations a thousand miles apart. Is this person a manic commuter? Is there "noise" on the databases that gets dates wrong? Or have computers conflated two people with the same name? This jumble of possible facts results from databases assembled using big data. Maybe we don't care most of the time if big data gets workplaces right for 80 percent of the people 95 percent of the time. That is not good enough for evidentiary purposes.

Even when not going to court but just looking at someone who is a candidate to be hired, big data is not enough. Public records for companies reveal very little about who works there. If databases tell us that someone has had three jobs in two years, we could wonder whether that person is a high-risk worker prone to quitting or getting fired. He could simply have been unlucky in working for companies that shut down just after he joined them. Or he could be even more unstable than he appears because we discover that four additional jobs were left off his résumé during that period.

Big data will not find us those omitted jobs. It will not account for what is not on the record. If you had been fired by a boss who hated you, you would surely prefer it if the name of that boss was never mentioned in your job interview. When handed any résumé, a careful hiring company should take the abductive approach. Big data has no place in this individualized inquiry.

—3—
INVESTIGATION: WHY YOU NEED IT
AND HOW TO GET STARTED

The real art of fact investigation has little to do with the source lists in the Appendices section of this book. Our biggest challenge as investigators is staying alert to—and thwarting—the tricks we play on ourselves to consider an investigation finished when it really is not. We need to be detectives the way the Cubists wanted viewers to approach their work. We need to be aware that answers will not come easily and that we may not see a full, intelligible picture that makes complete sense right away—or ever.

There is no "secret weapon" investigators have at their disposal. There is only the vast number of possible facts to be gathered and the faith we need to keep that an open-minded, systematic approach using intuition can raise the chances that we will get the information we need. Fact investigation beyond a casual Web search can seem daunting, but can yield great rewards.

INVESTIGATE FOR ASSETS BEFORE YOU SUE
AND IF YOU WIN

The argument for doing an investigation when it comes to identifying assets is easy. If someone has no money, a "win" against him in court is useless if there is nothing to collect. Sometimes you can be successful in court against a person or company with plenty of assets, only to be told four years later (after you get your judgment) that things have gone badly since the case was filed. Sadly, there is now nothing left for you, the victor.

Our firm had just such a case, in which a net worth statement of $12 million was enough to persuade our client to lend $5 million to a company that bought its building. The man who controlled the purchasing company also provided a personal guarantee to back up his company's promise to repay. When the buyer's company defaulted two years later, he was supposedly worth just $1 million personally and sought to negotiate his $5 million debt down by more than 80 percent.

We found that not only was he worth far more than $1 million, but that he had also failed to include lots of wonderful assets on the original net worth statement he provided to back up his guarantee. This provided great clues to expand our knowledge of his holdings. Like many people, he named his companies sequentially, so by including Alpha I LLC and Alpha II LLC on his net worth statement, we were able to check for and see that he owned Alphas III, IV, V and VI. All were still active and owned real property.

The trap our clients had fallen into was the "paint by numbers" syndrome described in Chapter 1, the idea that an assertion repeated enough times becomes indisputable fact. Because his net worth statement talked only about Alpha I and Alpha II, our clients wondered what was owned by *those* companies. Our question was, "What is owned by these and any other company controlled by the guarantor?" A fresh look at the man's net worth and our awareness that he would have had good reasons to omit a lot from his original statement (to make him seem judgment-proof later on) led us to look at him in a fresh way that presupposed nothing. (For more on how an asset search should proceed, see the very end of this chapter, below.)

INVESTIGATE TO HELP DISCOVERY GO FASTER

Many lawyers are trained to go after information using the most expensive method possible—the formal discovery process. Any litigator can tell you how expensive discovery is, and how slow. An added problem is that the process is predicated on the honesty of lawyers and their clients. You can ask for all relevant documents, but if you are not handed a relevant document you know nothing about, then what?

What's more, if you are permitting the opposing side to control nomenclature and names of key personnel, you probably have not investigated enough.

For example, it is not an exaggeration to say that two years of discovery requests for documents described as "the portion of the company dealing with default swaps" would be fought as overly vague, since these swaps could be originated, purchased, accounted for and audited by four different units. And unless you know the exact name of the individual department or, even better, the name of the person who would have been in charge of the department, it could be a long time before a judge would even hear arguments about whether documents are being unreasonably withheld.

In an ideal world we would want to conduct lots of depositions because statements in deposition are under oath, whereas interviews prior to the discovery process or even during it outside of the deposition setting are not. But the cost just will not allow lots of depositions much of the time.

Informal fact investigation is a lot cheaper than depositions, and the happy truth is that there are no time limits as there are in depositions. Calling 15 people to ask them about internal procedures and organization charts with names and functions of employees and departments could take a few days, but it will be far less costly than drafting interrogatories, reading responses and eventually deposing one or two people and hoping to find someone who will have something to say.

Former employees are a good place to start. Just as we like to find liabilities that lead to cash (see section on asset searching below), we like to talk to former employees to tell us about a company our clients are opposing today. Of course, current employees may know more about the company's operations, but they may be off-limits because of the no-contact rule (see the discussion of ethics, Chapter 5). Even if not off-limits, current employees may not make the best witnesses because they may be afraid of losing their jobs. In addition, the lawsuit could be about what happened at a company years before, when the former employees worked there.

Former employees can serve up all kinds of great information that will help with discovery. Who reported to whom? Can you help us fill out the Equity New Issues Desk organization chart? When there was a transaction over a certain limit that needed special approval, whose approval did you need? (Recall the real-life Problem 2 in the Introduction and its solution in the Appendix.)

INVESTIGATE TO GATHER FACTS DURING TRIAL

Any trial lawyer will tell you that there is never enough time to prepare for witnesses—either your own or the ones the other side will call. Trial lawyers need help. Here is what fact investigators can do:

- Impugn witness credibility. Sometimes lawyers have just a day or two to prepare. We once had a new witness in a bankruptcy hearing who claimed that he was happy to fund a bankruptcy plan for debtors he had met for the first time the previous day. Since this sounded unlikely, we decided to try to catch him in a provable lie, which we did in several hours of work. The mystery man claimed that neither he nor his companies were the subject of any ongoing litigation. Overnight, we found that several of his companies were involved in ongoing lawsuits, and the witness was confronted with the falsity of his testimony the next day.

- Analyze new evidence that arises during trial. One of the other side's witnesses in a case we worked on had consistently denied during discovery that he lived in a particular apartment building. Following him all the time was too expensive for our client. Instead, we periodically updated our database checks on him. He became careless and changed the electricity account for the apartment to his name, and this turned up in one of our subsequent checks. We then were then able to confirm his occupancy.

Investigate Nonlitigation Matters— Contracts, Mergers, Personnel

Human beings are terrible assessors of risk. Many of us have met people who will spend a year researching every possible cost and benefit to buying a $60,000 luxury car but will think nothing of investing the same amount of money in a public company's stock based on the recommendation of someone first encountered last week.

In the same way, companies are happy to risk $1 million in salary and benefits on an executive but balk at spending $2,000 to make sure he has told the truth on his résumé and—equally important—has not left out information that would cost him the job.

If you had bombed out in a job and were let go after two horrible months, would you list that position on your résumé as you looked for work three or five years later? "Checking references" means talking to people a job applicant wants you to talk to. The people to speak to are those the applicant *doesn't* want you to find and contact for a chat about that job that didn't last a long time.

CASE STUDY: DISASTER JOB SIX MONTHS AGO OMITTED FROM RÉSUMÉ

Our client was ready to hire a candidate for head of sales. He charmed everyone at the company as he described his 20-year career in business. Because the job was an important one for a new company, management team members knew they could ill afford to hire the wrong person. A "once-over-lightly" résumé checking service had confirmed some of the candidate's prior employment, but other jobs he had listed were accompanied by notations that said "called three times, no response." The applicant had no criminal record in his state of residence as well as the home state for this new job.

The man's unusual name returned a result in securities filings that included someone with his name being hired that same year by a publicly listed company. This job did not appear on his résumé. When we reported this to our client, who confronted the applicant, the applicant said that he had in fact worked at the public company for a short time but had been asked to perform unspecified unethical tasks. He had therefore chosen to omit the company from his résumé.

We searched filings and litigation records for the company that had hired the applicant earlier that year but found nothing suspicious. We then telephoned the president of this company and asked about the candidate. He had been fired for being ineffective and just plain lazy. "Whoever your client is, tell him not to make the same mistake I did," the president said. She had been warned by a prior employer that the applicant was charming in the interview stage and then did nothing once hired. "I disregarded that advice, but whoever is considering him now shouldn't make the same mistake," the president said.

Notice that when it comes to due diligence that demands anything more than robotic verification of a résumé or a criminal records check, it is impossible to come up with "proof" about a person's background. "Is he a good manager?" is not a question that can be answered using logic or statistics alone. All an investigator can do is to hand enough facts and interviews to clients so that they can be persuaded more likely than not of a particular trait the subject has.

No matter how much big data is available to be crunched by powerful computers, the answers about a specific person's personality need to be gathered one at a time. If that sounds a lot like what a jury does, that's because it is. If trial by database sounds awful to you, due diligence by database should too.

START WITH THE PUBLIC RECORD

The appendices to this book contain source lists of public records as well as some of the commercial databases available by paid subscriptions for legally permissible uses. The list is not exhaustive, and there is no correct order in which to search (more on this below). The main decisions to make at the outset are based on how much time you have for an investigation and whether you can afford to risk disclosing that the investigation is happening.

A former intelligence officer once said to me that the only way to be sure to preserve a confidence is "Don't tell anyone, and don't write it down." Because there is always a risk that an investigation will become public, I strongly recommend to our clients that any investigation begin with a quiet look at the public record. Unless I am in a great hurry or wish to have the person or company I am investigating become aware of the investigation (usually to exert pressure into settling a dispute), this is best practice.

By public record, we mean: every piece of paper or bit of electronic information we can gather about a person, be it in courthouses, land records, news stories, social media or commercial databases.

The reasons for starting with public documents are:

1. You may get only one chance to talk to a person, so make the best of the one interview you may have. You should be as well briefed as possible about what to ask. If you call someone on day one of an investigation, you may not ask about Theta LLC in Delaware because you haven't done enough research to uncover Theta LLC. Sometimes people are hard to reach. They can also be easy to find, but once they know why you are calling they may decide never to speak to you again. Sometimes, this can happen after they have talked to you for 30 minutes or more, after a friend or relative advises them to keep quiet and not talk to investigators working for attorneys.

2. Many investigations (especially asset searches) depend on secrecy. Anytime you pick up a phone and ask questions about a person, there is some chance that word of your call will get back to that person. This can happen even if you have called his sworn enemy. Any word that you are moving in on concealed assets could prompt the other side to shuffle the assets out of the company you found them in. You may still be able to find them later, but at much greater expense and with considerable loss of time.

A GOOGLE SEARCH IS NEVER ENOUGH

Investigation can be difficult. If it weren't, you would never need to hire someone to do it for you. Yet clients sometimes say to me: "You probably won't find much. We Googled him and didn't come up with anything."

What is wrong with this approach? Nearly everything. While Google is an indispensable tool for investigators, relying only on Google is like giving a carpenter just one tool—a sledge hammer—and saying, "Build me a house."

The most important reason Google is never enough is that most of the critical documents you need are not on Google. Google has not scanned and indexed all public records in the United States. Most U.S. counties (and many places in the rest of the world) require that to see public records, a person has to go down to the relevant government office and either make paper copies of whatever he needs or look on that agency's own computers that are not connected to the Internet.

Even information you find online may not be sufficient. Suppose you see on a county website that a company you suspect of being linked to your opponent bought a building. To find out who signed the mortgage on behalf of that company, you will usually be required to get down to the county records office and view the document for yourself—or, more commonly, send a record retriever to do it for you.

If you Google yourself, how much of your entire history, finances and associations will you find? Perhaps 1 percent. You will not see everyone you've ever worked with, all your limited liability companies, trusts and contractual obligations. If you have been to court in any capacity, you will probably not see a complete record of the cases relating to your appearance. And yet many lawyers supplement basic credit checks with nothing more than a Google search.

The second reason Google is not enough is that even though it is the best of the free search engines for now, it is not neutral like the index of an encyclopedia or the Library of Congress catalog. Google may employ computer scientists and library scientists, but Google is a business that favors those who advertise on it.

Google aims to deliver what it calls "quality" search results, but how does Google know what quality is important for you? Suppose the person you are investigating owns a chain of eight dry cleaners in two cities in Texas. He is a relative blip to Google because nobody links to the tiny dry cleaner company website. Perhaps the website tried advertising on Google but gave up. The owner's name is Smith and appears on page 23 of your Google search results.

So much for what Google thinks is "quality" for the purposes of your search.

Finally, a plain old Google search is insufficient because Google does not make the complex connections investigators have to make between two sets of facts, what some call "metasearching." The term refers to metasearch engines, which are programs that search *other* search engines to come up with a result. Using a metasearch engine is the Internet's version of asking a good reference librarian, "Where could I go to look up the following?"

Assume you want find an optician in Akron, Ohio, because he is a partner in the building you are financing. Is the optician working or suspended? Is he honest?

The first step is to ask, "Who licenses opticians in Ohio?" The answer found on Google is the Ohio Optical Dispensers Board. While Google has not indexed every optician in Ohio, what it has done is to index the indexes you need to find your person. You would then leave Google and go to the Optical Dispensers Board website to continue your search, where you may see whether your person has been suspended or reprimanded.

Then again, depending on the website, you may need to call the licensing authority, yet another step away from Google and even away from your computer keyboard to that old underused wonder, the telephone.

As dangerous as it is to rely solely on Google, it is also bad practice to skip a Google search altogether. But do not do just one. It is good practice to search Google at different times of the day and, if possible, from different locations. Google cares about word order, so you should vary that as well. Finally, using a local Google site will yield results you may never see at Google.com. Looking for a French company, use Google.fr and see the different results that appear.

THE INVESTIGATOR'S ENEMIES: CONFIRMATION BIAS AND THE SEMMELWEIS REFLEX

If you were told that the image in Figure 5 was that of a duck, you would probably see it right away. On the other hand, many people told to look at a rabbit in the same image would agree that it is in fact an image of a rabbit. The famous image is both, and is a useful reminder for an investigator that we often find that which we think we are seeking.[20]

Even after we know that we are looking at something unusual, this image is fascinating. While the information on the page never changes, we can see only a duck or a rabbit, but never both at the same time. We are just not able to take in at the same time two facts that we know to be mutually exclusive.

Investigation can feel like that too: In forming theories as we investigate, we gather evidence that may end up supporting what appear to be mutually incompatible conclusions. Our instinct is to favor the evidence that supports the conclusion we think is more likely, but we must resist that tendency. We will not find a man who is/is not bankrupt at the same time in the same jurisdiction (impossible), but we may find someone who was extremely wealthy in January and is broke in March.

Looking at the duck-rabbit takes more energy than looking at a conventional picture of a duck or a rabbit, because it clashes with our understanding of what kinds of animals exist on earth. A man who goes from riches to rags in six weeks will, similarly, be harder to investigate because we will have to overcome our own skepticism before we can consider the entire picture of events.

The tendency to find evidence to confirm the case we are trying to win is called confirmation bias, and lawyers are bursting with it. Lawyers are competitive by nature. Evidence they need is something they will naturally want to believe they have uncovered. Examples of this could be that since we "know" Robert Jones is strictly a "New York guy," we will not even look outside New York to see what else he may have done or acquired outside the state. In screening witnesses, we see that an expert witness has testified dozens of times, so we "know" he has no embarrassing personal history that could affect his credibility since "someone" is bound to have found it by now.

The flip side of confirmation bias is called the Semmelweis reflex, in which people ignore information that does not fit in with their world view. The reflex is named after Ignaz Semmelweis, a Viennese doctor who suggested that hand washing by doctors could reduce the chances that babies would die at birth. Doctors at the time would often come directly from dealing with cadavers and then deliver babies without washing their hands, because today's common knowledge about germs did not exist. Semmelweis was dismissed as a crank by those who "knew" that a gentleman's hands didn't get dirty. After doctors began washing their hands, infant mortality plunged.

Similarly, Samuel Arbesman in his remarkable book, *The Half-Life of Facts,* refers to "change blindness" or "inattentional blindness": When looking for one thing, we completely ignore everything else around us.[21]

EVEN CLIENTS GET THE NAME WRONG

Many subjects have unusual last names. Say you are looking through federal court records and see that someone with the same unusual last name as your subject but a different first name was involved in a massive civil suit in U.S. District Court last year. Could this be your subject, who uses only his middle name in business because he doesn't like anyone to know his hated first name? Or is it his brother and business associate? You will need to get the documents, read them and find out.

The same broadness of mind can help in other areas. Someone with an unusual last name lets you do better searches, so take advantage. If you think your subject may have been involved in an administrative proceeding brought by OSHA, do not search just OSHA but as many regulatory databases as you can. The same goes for securities records. There is such a wide array of forms at the SEC, I am always afraid I will miss something relevant if I try to guess which forms my person may appear on. If you can search on "all form" and "all dates," do so.

Your client may have briefed you on your subject, but based on faulty or incomplete information. Clients misspell names, they get dates wrong, and they confuse home and work addresses. Imagine you are searching for a person named Pelfrey in Michigan. Putting the name into a database could yield more than 5,000 results. Your client tells you Pelfrey lives in Lansing, but entering Pelfrey and Lansing comes up with no hits. But Pelfrey and Michigan gets the search down to 500 results, and you are in business. You find Pelfrey's father and brothers in entry 350, and find out that they used to live in DeWitt, Michigan, 14 miles from Lansing. Perhaps Pelfrey still lives there and your client was 14 miles off.

Even more difficult is when you are tasked with a number of different investigative goals. We were once asked to conduct a general background check of a European man. One of many things our client told us about him was that there were rumors that he could become involved in business with Iran, pending the loosening of sanctions by the United States. We found all the litigation we could that related to his companies, and read through a series of dull, low-value commercial disputes from years before.

On reading one lawsuit we thought could be useful to figure out the man's level of litigiousness, we noticed the port of embarkation of a shipment in dispute, and it became clear very quickly that our man was already a longtime trader with Iran. This was a facet of the investigation we had forgotten about and nearly overlooked because the facts of the dispute in the case before us were dull and turned on relatively little money.

THE INVESTIGATOR'S FRIEND: TIME LINES

From childhood bedtime stories to novels we read to ourselves as adults, people like stories. Despite the occasional flashback, the most gripping stories are the ones that happen in chronological order, just like real life. When an upset friend or relative tries to recount a jumbled series of facts—say a complicated argument over a complicated series of facts—we usually counsel them, "Go back, start at the beginning and tell me everything." What we mean by that is, "Give it to me in order."

Investigators do not have the luxury of finding out what they need to know in chronological order, but putting facts in order is not something to be done near the end of an investigation as you begin to draft your report. Putting events into context is an act that needs to happen every time we discover new information. Only when put it in its proper context can we maximize the information's value.

One technique I favor is to turn my notes into a chronology as soon as I've typed them up. The facts will probably be presented chronologically anyway, so the sooner they are put in order the better. And even if you are not typing up a full chronological memo for your client, a time line will help *you* make sense of the hundreds of facts you are gathering.

Say you are investigating Seller. He has decided to sell his business to Buyer, but there is no obvious reason for the prosperous Seller to do this. He is young, the business is not that old, and he is not getting a great price. You gather all kinds of information on Seller and find a ton of litigation. You see also that he has fully mortgaged his three homes and all of the equipment in his business. You put it all in a time line, and the story pops off the screen at you. Seller got sued by a client and settled, and right after that Seller mortgaged his equipment to Buyer. Two years later, Seller decided to sell his business to Buyer, but you might as well have called it a foreclosure.

Asset Searching: The Two Indispensable Elements

There are a lot of different reasons investigators get hired, but perhaps the most common request is for determining how wealthy an individual is. Getting ready to do an asset search is different in some ways from, for example, due diligence on the characteristics of a person you are considering hiring. For asset searches, we don't care what a person is like, and we don't care much whether he bought a house in 1999 and sold it for a 10 percent gain in 2002. What we care about is what he has *today*.

The most important principles of asset searches are:

1. If you haven't treated an asset search like a general background check, your search was too narrow. This may seem

to conflict with the statement above that we don't care about character when doing an asset search. However, we care about doing the same kinds of searches as we do when looking into character.

Information retrieval is not hierarchical. Today more than ever, it is easy to own things far from where you live or work. There may be categories in some of the databases that purport to give you lists of assets, but they are woefully inadequate. If these databases really did the job, why would anyone need help with asset searching? They would simply subscribe to these databases, plug in a person's Social Security number, and out would come the list they sought.

But databases miss a lot, never more than when they skip over companies controlled by individuals. The reason for this is simple. In most states (and of course in many tax havens the world over), people's names do not need to be linked on the public record to the name of their company. Once that link is broken, databases are stumped. Still, it can be reasonably quick work to connect the company and the person if the reason the company was set up was not for secrecy as much as to limit liability. (I make no secret that I own my Delaware limited liability company. I just don't want litigation opponents to be able to reach my savings account and my house.)

Hence, the need to do a more thorough background check when you are "only" looking for assets. Where does the subject live and work? Who owns those buildings? It could be that a company we find is owned by the very subject whose assets we are searching. Are there any companies associated with that address? What can we find out about those companies?

Look at Appendix IV, the questionnaire we give to matrimonial clients searching for assets controlled by an ex- (or soon-to-be ex-) spouse. In it we ask for all kinds of clues about pet names, names of summer vacation spots and anything else that could help us figure out what someone would name his company.

It takes some effort to come up with the name of a company that won't be traceable back to you and that has not already been taken. Many people don't bother to try picking such a name, because they set up companies to limit liability and not to hide assets. But years later, marriages or businesses go bad, and those companies are the first place a person thinks of to stash money away from the eyes of creditors.

Given how quickly and cheaply people can set up limited liability companies (and even ordinary corporations), it is folly to assume that a person who may be concealing assets would not have availed him or herself of this simple mechanism.

CASE STUDY: FINDING SIDE COMPANIES THROUGH A FAVORITE PROFESSIONAL

Many people use their own name or the name of their business when they start a company, and then tack on a number for the next company they form (Consolidated Parcels I, II, III etc.). But what happens when they pick an innocuous name that is not taken and has nothing to do with their own name, the name of their business or anything else about them? Think about a real estate developer from Atlanta named Daniel Frost. If he had a company called EuroAmerican Solutions, how would you find it?

We once had such a challenge, and noticed that our debtor always used the same lawyer to act as his registered agent. In that state, we were able to look up companies by registered agent. Even with a list of 300 or so companies to look through, we were able to isolate five that had names that may have related to our Daniel Frost. In running those company names through databases and public records, we were able to find that four of them were Frost's.

2.   If you haven't looked for liabilities as well as assets, your asset
     search was too restrictive.

"Asset" means something a little different to an asset searcher than it
would to an accountant. A proper asset search looks beyond everything
that would be on the "assets" side of a conventional balance sheet. While
the first item on a balance sheet is cash (part of "current assets"), we
usually spend little time looking for cash for the simple reason that cash
sitting in a bank account is extremely difficult to detect without a court
order.

Instead, it is better to start with things that you can *get* with cash.
Sometimes that helps us trace back to the source of the cash that bought
those things, and we find even more cash. This should be intuitive, but
is not because of the rush to find the cash itself. When you have an
asset, you've acquired it by exchanging something for it—usually cash
or the promise to pay back a loan. The balance sheet of a company or a
household won't tell you how the assets were acquired, but the cash flow
and income statements are meant to round out the picture. That is where
you get more detail about the buying and selling of things and where the
cash went.

When you borrow money to buy something, it is unusual to find that
asset completely underwater (this is, worth less than the money owed
to pay for it). If we find a mortgage, a UCC lien (more completely, an
Article 9 security agreement) or a mechanic's lien (usually money owned
to someone who worked on a house), we can often find the asset that
caused the liability to be incurred.

Assume a husband has a decent small business, and puts forward all
the financials for it in his negotiations for a separation agreement. A
valuation expert says the business is fairly valued and the wife's forensic
accountant can see nothing wrong with the books and records. A balance
sheet approach shows no real estate at all. But there is an operating lease
for the headquarters that is on both the income and cash flow statements.

It always pays to ask in such cases: Who is the landlord? Sometimes,
the landlord turns out to be the business owner in the form of a company

THE ART OF FACT INVESTIGATION

the other spouse did not know existed. A forensic accountant may assume without any other evidence that the landlord is an unrelated party. Yet, the landlord company owned by the moneyed spouse is an *asset* of that spouse. We just used the cash payments on the income statement of one company to get to an asset that is the secretly owned company.

Any time money is owed to someone and payment is not made (or there is a dispute about it), there is a greater chance of litigation. Therefore, litigation is always something to check in relation to any asset search. Our firm's list of assets found via a courthouse search is exhaustive:

- Antique cars that their owners did not register but were the subject of lawsuits because the owners fell behind on their storage bills.

- Apartments owned through shell companies that popped onto the record because the owners of the shell companies squabbled with real estate agents and did not pay their full bill. They were then sued personally as well as through the shell company.

- The spouse with an admittedly small share in a Wyoming ranch owned by his family, who turned out to have a larger share than he had told his wife. We found out about the inner workings of the family company that owned the ranch from one of the relatives who was left out and sued his brothers.

The first three chapters of this book discussed how to think about the searches we are doing, how to look for information and how to arrange what we find. We have referred many times until now to databases, the subject of the next chapter. Far from the magic bullets that some imagine, using these can be the most frustrating part of any investigation.

—4—
Databases: Powerful, Quirky,
So Often Wrong

All of the guesswork, intuition and creativity discussed so far in this book comes into play when dealing with databases. If people are quirky and unpredictable, why would the databases they design and maintain be any different? If you check your creativity or common sense at the door and expect the computer to do the work for you, your investigation will probably come to an unhappy and quick end (Figure 6).

We saw in the last chapter that as powerful as Google is, it is never enough to rely solely on Google if you are doing a thorough search on a person or company. Some people understand that. Yet when they ask our firm to help them, many assume we can easily overcome the Google problem with databases at our disposal.

Some of the databases we use are subscription-only services that collate public records with bits of information from credit reports and other commercial sources. Others are freely available on the Internet but can be difficult to use when navigating them for the first time.

As with Google, these databases are necessary but not sufficient to do most jobs. On the most basic level, databases don't cover everything we want. The next time you are searching in a paid database, you may notice a little question mark somewhere around the box where you enter your search terms. Click on that and prepare to be shocked.

"Nationwide" coverage of marriage licenses may include only a handful of states, because such licenses are not public information in many jurisdictions. In other cases, the information is public but the database doesn't include it because it's too expensive to gather data that has not been scanned and stored electronically. In such cases, you need to send someone to the courthouse.

Sometimes, for very simple questions, the answer we want is available in the databases: Where does John Hawkins live? What is his cellphone number? Does he have a criminal record in a particular state (assuming we have his correct date of birth)?

But for even mildly complex questions, the human brain is still a required element in coaxing the answers we want out of the billions of unverified facts in electronic storage. Part of the reason is, as we saw in Chapters 1 and 2, investigation is a matter of guesswork and intuition. Computers do not guess and cannot "know" what we are looking for. For example, Watson, the computer that won on the television game show "Jeopardy!," didn't know that it won its game because it was just manipulating formal symbols input by human beings, noted philosophy professor John Searle.

"Watson did not understand the questions, nor its answers, nor that some of its answers were right and some wrong, nor that it was playing a game, nor that it won — because it doesn't understand anything," Searle wrote.[22]

Who Owns This Building?

To illustrate the difficulty of using databases without keeping your brain fully engaged, I tried the following exercise on three successive classes of law school students taking a "Fact Investigation" course. Not one provided the complete answer.

The database in question was one of the simplest to fathom. The question was "Who owns the building we are sitting in right now?" The multistory building was in a city in which every deed and mortgage is scanned online and freely available via a website. What could be simpler?

It turned out that when students entered the address of the building in the database of deeds, they were met with a "cannot complete your request" message because the structure was a condominium. Each individual floor is registered separately as an individual lot, and without the lot number, the database would not provide the ownership information.

Most of the students returned with the assignment unfinished. Some would get part of the building's ownership based on website searching, but would not get an exhaustive list of each floor's owner since the owners of some floors did not have websites. In addition, without being able to crack the database, we had no way of knowing whether some floors were divided among several owners.

To finish this assignment, the students needed to think creatively. The answer to the question was one that struck me as obvious: If you don't know the lot number, enter "1" and see what happens. One wonderful thing about databases is that it is impossible to break them by asking for the wrong information. If the search is free, there is no downside to experimentation.

In this case, entering "1" invited a list of all the lot numbers in the building. It turned out that the ground floor was lot 1001, the second floor 1002, and so on.

Of course, this approach will not work on every database. Some will require the exact lot number, and you may therefore need the assistance of a human being from the county clerk's office. The lesson for the students doing this exercise was that for even the simplest of searches, turning on a computer does not allow you to turn off the part of your brain that is not like a computer—the part that uses intuition with no firm factual basis for doing so.

MORE DATA, BUT NOT MORE SHARING

The most common problem in using databases is that the information you want simply isn't there, for the same reason it is not on Google: It is not posted on the Internet, and therefore the databases do not pick it up.

Another problem nearly as common is that databases frequently are very bad at talking to one another and sharing what they know.

Poor communication is a failing common with people, who just happen to be the ones who set these databases up. In his book, *The Half-Life of Facts,* Samuel Arbesman discusses the finding of physicist and library science professor Don R. Swanson, who wrote about the bad organization of knowledge. Swanson's work demonstrated that individual bits of knowledge that were uncontroversial were not fully penetrating academia. As a result, researchers remained unaware of information that could help them.

As Arbesman summarized, if there was a paper showing that A implies B, and somewhere else a journal article showed that B implies C, "since no one has read both papers, the obvious result—that A implies C—remained dormant."

This kind of thing happens a lot more than we realize,[23] according to Swanson.

Thus, the question "which databases do you use" is an appropriate one to ask a potential investigator but does nothing to tell you how good that investigator is. Good investigators are the ones who know databases are but a starting point. For example, two newspaper databases may not index the same papers. If you are looking for information on a Korean-American around New York City, chances are neither newspaper database will index the Korean papers in New York or New Jersey. Clicking on the definition of an "all languages" search reveals on one database that "all" really means "16." Korean is not among them, so even Chosun Ilbo, one of the largest-circulation papers in South Korea, will not be indexed in Korean or even its English edition.

People need to help databases talk to one another. If one database links an address to a person, not all of them will. Feed just an address into other databases to see what comes up. A home address may link to your man on one database, but on another may link to his (so far) secret company.

Databases Are Like the New Boss

Most of us who have worked for someone for any length of time know that to get something from a particular boss, you have to prepare the paperwork/presentation/request just so. Some bosses like to be briefed in a certain way before they make a decision. Some want lots of paperwork as backup. Others want bullet points only. Databases are this way too, because they are programmed by the same maddeningly idiosyncratic people we deal with every day.

Assume your subject's company is called Arbor Beauty Supply Corp. You look this company up on the Pennsylvania Secretary of State website and there it is, with the county it's registered to, the name of the agent for service of process and possibly a fictitious name as well.

Are you done investigating the owner of Arbor Beauty Supply? No, because if you enter just "Arbor Beauty" into the database you find results that include Arbor Beauty Real Estate LLC, Arbor Beauty Automotive Holdings LLC and Arbor Beauty Partners LLC. Do these belong to your subject too? Might they be the companies that hold his real estate, fleet of cars and other assorted businesses?

Now shift the hunt to Connecticut, which is fussier about search terms. If you enter "Arbor Beauty" the computer may tell you there is no such company in existence. That is because Connecticut often demands that you put in most or all of the company's name every time.

There is no secret to knowing the difference between databases. You have to use them to get to know them, just as you have to work with people for a time before you get to know *them*.

Databases Make Mistakes

People make a lot of mistakes, and so do databases. If someone you are investigating has a name that has multiple possible spellings, you should enter those into the database as well. A good investigator is better than the clumsy data-entry clerks of this world. If you are looking for Robert, check out Bob, Rob, Robbie, Bobbie and even Robt.

If a person's name is Wang Li, his last name is most likely Wang. However, you need to take into account that not everyone knows that. If he is in the United States, he will be filed as Mr. Li in half a dozen places. In addition, you would be smart to check Wong Lee, Li Wong, Wang Lee and Lee Wang.

A very useful source of name spellings is the Social Security Death Index at Ancestry.com and elsewhere. If a witness tells you a man's name but isn't sure how it's spelled, this index can get you most every possible spelling since it indexes almost everyone who has lived and died in the United States in the past 70 years. This proved helpful to me once when I was looking for a former employee of a company who had a long Italian name with three possible double or single consonants and two syllables that could have contained an A, I or O. Once I had a few new likely combinations to work with, I found that man in 15 minutes on a paid database.

KEEP ALL WINDOWS OPEN

One of the first questions a new investigator tends to ask is, which database comes first? We like to start with the basic ones that tell us where a person has lived for the past few years, but after that there is no good answer.

Think of each database like a window on your PC (or a tab on your browser). Once you get into that database, you may need to go back to it again and again during the investigation. Even if you manually log out of it and close the window, think of all your databases as open windows that you may not close until the investigation is complete.

For neatness enthusiasts, this is maddening. They want to check "securities filings," off their list and move on. The danger in moving on too quickly is that we learn many things during the course of an investigation. If we check securities filings for Roger Walter Corcoran and his two known companies on the first day of the investigation, should we not check again if two weeks later we find out that Corcoran has another company we did not know about that first day? What if we find out in an interview that he likes to be called "Walt" Corcoran? The only responsible thing is to go back to the "window" that is the securities database and look again.

Doing multiple searches means that a well-organized investigation keeps a record of what has been searched and when. Usually the broader the search the better, which can mean a fairly long search string such as [Roger/2 Corcoran or "Walt Corcoran" or "Corcoran, Inc." or "84562 Garden Ln."] If you discover a new company late into the investigation, you may not remember the following day which databases you ran it through. If you have a simple system that puts the search string, database and date searched in one place, you will know when it is time to go back to an open window and run a search a second time.

Figuring out a search string can involve trial and error inspired by guesswork. It is the most delicate part of an investigation after doing interviews. The right search string can be the difference between "No Results" and "Search returned more than 10,000 results, please narrow search terms."

I was once asked to explain to a client's litigation department how we had established a link between an opposing party and a third person with a similar family name but spelled differently than the opposing party's name.

The third person claimed that the opposing party had breached a valuable contract, and the opposing party sued our client for damages. The two men had extremely common Middle Eastern names, so doing a press search on both of them instantly returned more than 5,000 entries. However, one of the men lived in a small city in the United States. Entering his name and the name of the city produced no results. We then broadened the search gradually until the name of the man and the state produced 600 hits in the LexisNexis media database. In our experience, that is a reasonable number to look through, and we began digging in.

Within an hour, we had our answer: an obituary for the opposing party's father, who lived in a different part of the state from the opposing party, revealed that the two men with similar last names were in fact brothers.

Another useful search string technique is to run a 'bad word search" on a person, especially in cases of due diligence. Think of every word you can that would be included in a newspaper story about someone you would not want to hire. Theft, embezzle, larceny, fraud, harassment, assault. Run all of those with the common name of the person you are investigating and you will immediately weed out all of the high school football results and zoning board reports that populate the media databases. Those results are fine in some kinds of investigations, but in others they clog up the process.

For a starter list of databases see Appendix II.

—5—
How to Investigate
Legally and Ethically

Fact investigation may be an art, but a lawyer's "artistic license" is limited by legal and ethical considerations that prevent us from doing whatever it takes to get the information we need.

Often, those who have had a bad experience when using investigators found that the investigator used poor judgment or failed to follow instructions. For example, poor judgment may mean you failed to rerun a database search with new information or failed to check the courthouse for a lawsuit that was not available online.

Far more serious lapses are committed by investigators who break the law or those who obey the law but still trample the rules of professional ethics that bind both lawyers and everyone who works for those lawyers.

The easiest way to eliminate an investigator from a list of candidates is to run a few ethical or legal issues by him or her. Many will provide the wrong answer without knowing it. We regularly get calls from lawyers who are incredulous that we cannot get quick access to a person's banking records without a court order. "My last investigator did it," they sometimes tell us. We are polite, but wonder whether they are calling us because their last investigator is in prison. As we will see in this chapter, this does happen.

THE AGENCY PRINCIPLE

If a lawyer hires an investigator, the investigator is that lawyer's agent. That does not mean the lawyer is allowed to hide his eyes and let the investigator proceed in any way the investigator wants.

Under the rules of professional ethics, lawyers have an explicit duty to supervise their agents to make sure that those agents adhere to the ethical rules.[24]

Even if the lawyer had no actual knowledge of an agent's misdeeds, courts can still find that lawyer liable. In Stephen Slesinger Inc. v. Walt Disney Company,[25] a fight over royalties related to Winnie the Pooh, Slesinger hired an investigator to obtain Disney documents to support its case. Slesinger gave no supervision to the investigator, but did instruct the investigator that everything the investigator did should be legal.

The investigator proceeded to take thousands of pages belonging to Disney by breaking into a number of Disney office buildings and secure trash receptacles. The record also states that the investigator trespassed onto the facility of a company Disney had hired to shred its confidential documents. The documents were passed on to Slesinger's attorneys.

The case is notable for the punishment the court exercised on the plaintiffs who had hired the investigators. Instead of merely excluding the illegally obtained evidence or sanctioning the attorneys, the court *dismissed the entire case*. The court's reasoning was that even if the plaintiffs initially told the investigators to obey the law, based on the results the investigators produced the plaintiffs had to know their investigator was breaking the law.

Other times, investigators acting improperly have not destroyed their client's entire case. But lawyers whose investigators produced cellphone records from opposing parties and who never asked how the phone records were obtained have been subjected to punitive damages on a claim of intrusion.[26]

The most famous recent case of a rotten investigation was that of Anthony Pellicano, the Los Angeles-based "investigator to the stars." He worked for some of the biggest names in show business and their lawyers and was known for his willingness to use any tactic to get the information his clients wanted. When the late billionaire Kirk Kerkorian hired entertainment lawyer Terry Christensen during a nasty custody dispute, Christensen hired Pellicano.

Pellicano illegally tapped the phone of Kerkorian's estranged wife, and went to jail after being convicted in 2008. Christensen was also sentenced to prison time for hiring a criminal enterprise. He appealed, but his sentence was upheld.[27]

Information Forbidden Without a Court Order

Clients often ask whether we can get them information that is off-limits. The three main types of information that are forbidden without a court order yet are still highly sought-after are:

- Bank account numbers, balances and activity records (protected by the Gramm-Leach-Bliley Act).[28]

- Medical records (protected by HIPAA).[29]

- Telephone records (protected by the Telephone Records and Privacy Protection Act of 2006).[30]

Most of the time, investigators who obtain forbidden information do not go to the lengths of the people in the Slesinger case. Many do not get caught, as they were in the Pellicano case. With a computer and a telephone, investigators can trick banks and phone companies into handing over information. The way it is done—again, in violation of federal law—is to pretend to be the person whose records you are trying to obtain. If you know something about him, including Social Security numbers, his mother's maiden name or other phone numbers, it is surprisingly easy to "pretext" your way into getting information that is off-limits.

What is upsetting is the brazenness with which many investigators approach the task. Cellphone records are for sale on the Internet. Reminder: Obtaining them is *not* a legitimate business. Companies will tell you they can get banking information legally, but usually through a "proprietary" process that remains a secret. You depend on them not to use pretexting, but you still have a duty to know how they do what they do.

WHEN DOES DISSEMBLANCE STOP AND PRETEXTING BEGIN?

Whether to pretend to be someone you are not is an easy call when there is a clear law forbidding the practice, as in the categories in the previous section. But what about being vague as to the purpose of your inquiry? Assume you contact the former employee of a bus company to ask about the boss to whom the former employee remains loyal? If you tell him exactly why you want to talk to him and who your client is (someone suing that ex-boss for lots of money), he will probably hang up the phone on you.

Most of us are raised with the idea that lying is a bad thing. As we get into the workplace, we learn words such as "dissembling" that are polite ways of describing speech that misleads but falls short of what may be called a lie.

Lying is sometimes illegal (most commonly we associate it with "fraud" of the civil or criminal variety). There are also criminal impersonation statutes. In New York, for instance, criminal impersonation happens when you pretend to be someone else with the intent to defraud, or when you claim to be the representative of an organization that you are not.[31] Even more serious is impersonating a police officer.[32]

If every untruth that was uttered subjected the speaker to litigation, the courts would be stuffed to the point of breakdown. Still, lawyers have a special duty not to lie.[33] The hard question is, when does dissembling become lying? Black's Law Dictionary defines "dissemble" as: "To give a false impression about (something); to cover up (something) by deception (to dissemble the facts)." Many state bar associations struggle with the distinction.[34]

Many jurisdictions make an exception to their no-lying rule in matters of intellectual property[35] or race discrimination related to housing. It is difficult to see how any such investigations could proceed unless someone can pretend to be looking for a house to rent or what he knows to be a counterfeit piece of merchandise to buy. In the same way, process servers are given more latitude than attorneys in being allowed to stretch the truth when they need to get into a building or lure someone to the door to serve them with a summons or subpoena. In criminal defense matters, lawyers can be given more latitude than those working on civil matters.[36]

Pretexting can be even more problematic when dealing with social media. In the early days of Facebook, lawyers had no opinion on inventing a false identity with which to "friend" someone on Facebook.

The first casualty of the anti-pretexters in the bar associations were the people who, instead of pretending to be a real individual, made up a person out of whole cloth. A photo of an anonymous person with a fake name, school pedigree and job would often be accepted as a "friend" of the target person on Facebook, giving the lawyer in control of the phony person access to the target's other friends as well as postings (which might include phone numbers, travel plans and more). This information was intended to be available only to friends and not the general public.

Fake personas soon became frowned upon, so lawyers decided to "dissemble" when it came to the Web. They would use a relative or an administrative assistant from their firm or someone else to contact and "friend" the key person. No lies would be told about the identity of the person putting out the friend request, but the purpose of the request — finding out information related to litigation—would be suppressed.

This kind of practice began to change in 2009, when the Philadelphia Bar Association decided that omitting the purpose of the approach on Facebook was deceptive and tantamount to the making of a false statement, and therefore disallowed.[37]

For the writers of this opinion, using false statements to gain access to private communication is no different than pretending to be a utility worker in order to gain access to a private home for the purpose of installing a hidden camera. On the other hand, videotaping people as they walk around in public is likened to looking at the public, unprotected portion of someone's Facebook account.

Different state and local bar associations have different interpretations of how much dissembling may be allowed in approaching a person over social media, and the New York City Bar disagrees with Philadelphia's.[38]

What is clear is that the careful investigator will know the case law and the ethics rules for the area in which he works. Approaching the issue from the point of view of what nonlawyers can get away with means taking an unnecessary risk.

THE NO-CONTACT RULE

A big adjustment for some investigators who used to be reporters is that if you are a lawyer (or are working for a lawyer on any job), there are some people you are just not allowed to talk to. While it is not the case that you would be breaking the law if you talked to them, you would be violating a basic rule of a lawyer's professional responsibility, known as the no-contact rule. Rules that govern the conduct of lawyers may also have an effect on evidence: Gather something that violates the rules, and that evidence could be thrown out of your case.[39]

The no-contact rule (Rule 4.2 in the ABA's Model Rules) restricts the ability of a lawyer or the lawyer's agents from communicating with a party who is represented by another lawyer about the subject of the representation.

What that often means for an investigator is that if your client is suing Mr. Jones, you may not call up Mr. Jones and talk to him without his lawyer being on the phone unless the lawyer has given permission ahead of time, or if there is a court order allowing the communication. If you are searching the assets of a represented company, employees of that company may also be off-limits.[40]

Low-level employees may not fall under the no-contact rule, but conservative practice dictates that current employees should be left alone. Even if they had nothing to do with the matter at the center of litigation, it could take several minutes of conversation to establish that that they are fair game for an interview. During those minutes you may discover a fact that muddies the water or forces you to conclude that they are indeed subject to the no-contact rule. If it's a close call, you may need to go to court to have the judge hear a motion about whether to allow a conversation with a particular employee. That is an expense most clients would think very carefully about bearing.

Fortunately, former employees of the company are fair game, which is often the best place to start since they will usually be more likely to chat than people still afraid for their jobs and the reputation of their current employer.

One of the most useful reasons to talk to former employees is to build an organization chart of a company opposed to you in litigation. Say that in discovery you demand documents that relate to "the computer system" used by the large company in question. The response could be something to the effect of, "We have seven different systems, so this request is overly broad." You are back to having to ask again, but how can you specify which system to ask about when you don't know which systems the company uses? The answer could be: Find someone who worked there until six months ago. A former employee would know about the computers, especially if you find someone from the information technology department.

To be properly cautious, when calling former employees you need to make sure they really are former employees. If a database or social media seems to indicate they used to work at the company but in fact are still there, then you may have violated the no-contact rule. Your obligation is to make sure they really are former employees before you begin a substantive interview. If they still work there, apologize and hang up.

RECORDING PHONE CONVERSATIONS

The United States presents a patchwork of philosophies over the question of recording telephone conversations. Some are "one-party" states, which means that you can record a conversation as long as one person on the call consents. In one-party states, investigators and lawyers can legally record conversations without the knowledge of the people they are recording. Some states are "two-party" jurisdictions, which means that all parties on a call need to know that a recording is taking place. In that event, an investigator and a subcontractor working for him may not record a conference call with a third person without that third person's knowledge. In no state can you freely record a conversation if none of the participants know you are recording them—that would be a violation of federal wiretapping laws, which require a court order before a tap is put in place.

But even if you are sitting in a one-party state, you need to be careful about recording your conversation. If the other person on the call is not in the one-party state with you, then you may be subject to the laws of the state that other person is in. Usually, without asking, you have no way of knowing for certain where the person on the other end of the call is. It is now common to have an office number that forwards to a cellphone. Even if you call the landline of a New York office building, you may actually be calling California, which requires the consent of all parties before you can lawfully record a conversation.

For lawyers, the terrain is more complex because recordings that are legal may still be held by their state bars to be unethical. In New York, for instance, the professional bias among lawyers is that in general lawyers should not record conversations.

"PINGING" CELLPHONE SIGNALS

A more clear-cut issue is "pinging" cellphones, which uses a phone's global positioning system (GPS) to determine its location. While there are commercial applications you can buy to track your own phone, pinging someone else's phone (usually by triangulating the cellphone tower signals it picks up) is sometimes used by law enforcement or other government agencies in certain limited circumstances to locate individuals who have called emergency services or are otherwise being sought by the police.

Despite the claims by some investigators that pinging without a court order is commonplace, it is still illegal for investigators to get someone in the phone company to ping for them.[41]

GPS Tracking Devices

In most U.S. jurisdictions, the ability of the government to place GPS tracking devices on someone's car is restricted. For the government, the Supreme Court held in U.S. v. Jones[42] that the attachment by law enforcement of a GPS tracking device to a vehicle and then using the device to monitor the vehicle's movements constitutes a search under the Fourth Amendment. For that, you need a search warrant.

Non-law enforcement purposes by government are less clear-cut. For instance, in Cunningham v. New York State Department of Labor, New York's highest court held that a state government agency's attaching a GPS device to a state employee's car needs no search warrant, but the search must be reasonable. [43] More recently, the state's stalking statute was amended to include the use of GPS tracking. However, to be liable the person being stalked has to tell the stalker that his or her behavior is unwelcome.[44]

A lawyer who wants to play it safe should make sure the person authorizing placement of the tracking device is the owner of record of the car the device will be going onto.

Mirror Imaging Hard Drives

Computers can be a gold mine of information, but they can be a snake pit of liability if you help yourself to information to which are not entitled.

The key distinction when it comes to computers is authorized access versus real-time interception of computer activity by spyware that monitors and records the activities of other people without their knowledge. That kind of evidence is usually inadmissible and obtaining it may be a felony as well.

If clients ask us to copy and analyze a computer drive used by their spouse, we always want to know whose computer we are being asked to examine. If this is the spouse's computer but not our client's, we will not touch it. If it is a shared computer, we have language in our engagement letter that puts the burden on the clients: they assert that they have the right to the computer.

We heard one horror story by a divorce lawyer and investigator about a computer that the wife asserted was used by all members of the family. The husband denied this, and said the computer was owned by his business and that it contained trade secrets. The evidence on the computer became the subject of lengthy and expensive hearings about whose computer this really was.

A more cautious approach that can avoid some legal and ethical headaches is this: If you have a reasonable basis to think you have the right to copy a computer, copy it but do not look at the contents. Preserve it with proper custody and labelling as you would other kinds of evidence, and then let a judge decide if you may examine the contents. If the answer is no, then you cannot be accused of causing major damage in any invasion of privacy claim.

−6−

INTERVIEWING: WHERE INVESTIGATORS EARN THEIR MONEY

The interview stage of an investigation can be the most rewarding part of the whole process. So much information is not written down at all, whether a country has a high level of computer use or is barely online. And of the portion of the world's information that is recorded on paper or a hard drive, a lot of it is not on the public record.

Many an investigation can get stalled once the public record and databases have been exhausted. You can collect every available document on someone—every business they've had, every court case, every newspaper article that mentions them—and then reach the point at which only talking to someone about that person will yield anything more.

As with the "Google yourself" exercise in Chapter 3, compare what you know about yourself with what is written down in any public medium—everywhere you have ever worked, ever traveled, every person you've ever met. In addition, certain things tend not to be written about people at all unless they are already well known. What is this person like to work with? No database will have that kind of information. For this, you should locate former colleagues and then ask them about your subject.

Like starting a business, leveraging property investment or moving to a new country to start a new life, the potential greater reward of doing an interview carries greater risk. The investigation could go public and spark a cover-up. Or, the person being investigated could alert close friends and colleagues not to talk to the investigator. That first interview could be your last.

Interviewing requires the same mindset the Cubists wanted in their viewers and that this book argues is needed to perform a good investigation—curiosity and being open-minded to alternate truths. The well-known rule among litigators "Never ask a question to which you don't know the answer" may be fine for court or depositions, but that kind of questioning is not the best course of action for a fact investigator.

Because we know so much *less* than we think, over-preparing to the point of anticipating answers will make an interviewer less alert to any surprises that may emerge. Just as we take a fresh approach to each person when we do a public-records check, we need to keep in mind those public records when we start our interview yet be fully aware that the public record is at best a rough abstraction of someone's life. It can be more accurate than what someone tells you (if that person has a bad memory or tells lies). Yet sometimes the public record turns out to be badly out of date or just plain wrong.

If a client is going to be anywhere from disappointed to furious with an investigator, it will most likely come to pass over the interview stage. Some who have used investigators in the past are afraid to hire another one, often because the investigators departed from the rules of ethics once they were given clearance to pick up a phone and talk to someone.

TEMPLATES: GOOD PROTECTION FOR INVESTIGATORS AND THEIR CLIENTS

Templates help to ensure that an investigator and client are agreed on how much the interviewer may reveal about the reason for the investigation.

Some of the key questions you want answered by the template include:

- How will the interviewer represent him/herself? Lawyers and their agents are not allowed to lie, so your investigator may not pretend that he represents the Gallup poll or The New

York Times. He should give his real name even if it is only his first name. Of course, calling up a stranger and saying "This is Peter and I'd like to talk to you about your old roommate" will invite a quick hang-up from many people, but such is the tradeoff between vagueness and effectiveness. Giving the name of the investigator's firm or company will help.

- Why will the interviewer say he is calling? Is he allowed to identify you, the client? If not, how much can he say? Is he allowed to say his client is a lawyer? These are questions that should be discussed with the investigator ahead of time. The answers are committed to a template that both sides agree will be used.

- If the interview will be in person, what is the composition of the team that will be sent? Two men can seem more intimidating than a male-female team. Do you have permission to approach the subject without notice, perhaps after he or she has failed to return a number of phone calls?

Doing a template protects the lawyer who hires the investigator because if the investigator exceeds his authority and starts telling a subject something not on the template, the lawyer can at least argue that the investigator violated strict instructions to abide by the template.

Templates can also protect the investigator if the subject says too much and later argues that he was duped into speaking. As long as the template has been approved by the client and does not cross that line between dissembling and fraud, the investigation should be on solid ground.

Be Nice, Be Conversational

There are plenty of how-to books about interviewing. Given that, here are some general guidelines for lawyers seeking to do their own interviews or hiring someone to do it for them. It comes from the perspective of someone who worked as a journalist before becoming a lawyer.

The most important advice for lawyers and former police officers attempting to interview people who are not compelled to speak is this: **Be nice to them.**

Niceness is not the same as the polite form of address that lawyers use in depositions. Nice is definitely *not* the interrogation-type of address some police officers use when speaking to a suspect. Do not be accusatory or threatening. Refrain from using profanity.

Being nice to people is treating them the way you would like to be treated. "Is this a good time to speak?" or "I don't want to take up too much of your time." "If you're undecided about speaking to me because you don't know my company, would you like to research it and let me call you back tomorrow or the next day?"

While this approach is not suitable all the time for every subject, it works extremely well when the person you wish to speak with will not benefit from having the conversation. The worst thing to do if you want people to talk to you is to make them think you are demanding information.

For example, if you wish to figure out whether Mr. X is a member of Vega LLC, you call Mrs. G who used to work there, and you have a few choices on how to start:

1. "Mrs. G, I'm an attorney and I am thinking of suing Mr. X, a man you worked with at Vega LLC in November 2012. If you have two hours, at some point I would like to find out everything you know about Mr. X. When may we do this?"

This is unlikely to work. Why should Mrs. G be bothered? She could be good friends with Mr. X; she could be indifferent to Mr. X but dead set against class action suits of any kind. You have no idea.

OR:

2. "Mrs. G, my name is [your real name here] and I work for [your real company here]. We do fact investigation and research work in [your city

here], and we had a client who was interested in finding out a little more about Mr. X. I was under the impression that you worked with him at Vega back in 2012. Do you have a few minutes to talk with me?"

The second sounds better, does it not? You are conversational, you are not demanding a lot of time, and you have not breathed the word "litigation." Of course, this approach has downsides: Some will not talk to people with unnamed clients and vague goals. Some people avoid talking to strangers. Some will demand to know the name of your client, and if you are not authorized to tell them your client's name, they will hang up on you.

Start Low and Work Up

One way to get around the hang-ups is to start low and work your way up in a company's organization chart. The more senior the person, the more afraid of litigation he or she will be, and the more likely to have a lawyer on speed dial to consult before speaking to anyone. The former assistant bookkeeper, receptionist or intern may be the person you want to start with. The worse they were treated at the company, the more they will be happy to tell you what you want to know.

Consider some of the most high-profile criminal investigations in the United States in recent decades. In both the Bernard Madoff scandal and the collapse of Enron, the most senior people fell last (other than Madoff, who just confessed when he knew his Ponzi scheme was collapsing). Lower-level people had less to lose (and gained deals for reduced sentences) by speaking to the authorities. Prosecutors kept going up the chain of command until Madoff's top deputies and Enron CEO Kenneth Lay themselves faced charges—sometimes years after the initial arrests.

Start in a General Way

It's best to begin your interview with an easy question. If you were to strike up a conversation with a stranger in a train or at the gate at an airport, you would not begin by asking him about something difficult, awkward or controversial. Interviews may not need to start with "Do you live in St. Louis, or is this a business trip?" But starting with "Which executives were to blame for that corporate collapse?" risks a quick termination of the phone call.

Back to Mrs. G, who you hope will tell you about Mr. X at Vega. You want to know how powerful Mr. X was at the company. Working closely with the CEO would be a sign that he may have had clout there. If your first question is "Did he work closely with the CEO?" and the answer is no, you may have brought things to a close before Mrs. G can settle in and start to trust you. Better to start with something inoffensive and general that can lead to where you want to go.

"What was he like to work with?" Or perhaps, "Who did he work with there?" is better. Notice we do not say "With whom did he work?" This is not a deposition, and the spirit of the random chat at an airport gate should discourage unduly formal language.

Check Your Ego at the Door

The interview is meant to *gather* information, so check your ego at the door. If it will make it easier to gather information by pretending you know less than you do, then that is what you should do.

If Mrs. G starts by talking about how great Mr. X was at organizing the company Christmas party, do not cut her off. Let her tell you what is important to her. You could then turn that answer toward something you might need. "That's a lot of work on the Christmas party for one guy," you might say. "Were his colleagues or bosses OK with that?" Then Mrs. G might say, "Sure, he and the CEO were very close, so who would complain?" Or she might say, "He was so low-level nobody in the C-Suite would ever notice if he was away from his desk for a month."

The worst thing you could do would be to interrupt Mrs. G and say, "I already know about the Christmas party. Anything else?" That would convey the impression that Mrs. G has no choice but to sit there and be interrupted, whereas she has the option of hanging up the phone. It also tells her that you may not be the innocent "just a few questions" kind of person you hinted at in your opening.

After a bit, Mrs. G tells you that Mr. X is very close to CFO Kelly, someone you happen to want to investigate as well. You could say, "Oh, I know all about Mr. Kelly. Mr. Kelly is the guy who manages all the money there."

Instead, when Mrs. G. mentions Kelly, you could ask: "Is that Kelly with an E-Y or just Y? What's his first name? And he's the CFO, you say?" Simple, but Mrs. G won't be on alert that you're a sharp questioner with a stack of research about Mr. Kelly, Mr. X (and maybe even Mrs. G herself) sitting right in front of you.

You should also not be afraid to leave the subject of Kelly and then come back to him a bit later in the conversation. You will not be docked points if you pull a Columbo and say you forgot to ask one thing about Kelly earlier. In fact, it will make you seem like what you want to seem like: a normal person just like Mrs. G.

Because it is human nature to think we know more than we do, the idea that you are an open book and are willing to hear what these people have to say could surprise you with information you did not have. Pretending you know less than you do will help to remind you that you probably *do* know less than you think you do.

Many is the investigation that turns on a quick remark. Before you know it, you are asking Mrs. G how to spell the name of the person you have never heard of until the minute she uttered it, and you are asking not for effect but because you have uncovered a lot of new information.

Best of all, by getting this information well before depositions, you are way ahead of the game and may have saved tens of thousands of dollars.

Special Caution for Searching in Small Towns

If you are poking around in a small town, your request about some of your subject's public records could get right back to him—thanks to the friendly courthouse clerk who knows everyone. For small-town searches, consider hiring someone from a different state to make the information request.

Say Harry and Willa are divorcing and live in a small county. If a request was made by an out-of-state researcher for court documents about Harry, two of his neighbors and two randomly selected people on another street in the town, it would not be as obvious that Willa's lawyer is doing an asset search as it would be if the request came in for information about Harry alone.

–Appendix I–
Answers to Problems from Introduction

Answer to Problem 1

We started on this case as we always do with any investigation—by assuming nothing. In pulling together every single public record we could find about the subject, Mr. A, we quickly found something that had eluded the journalists who had written about him: He was not Italian at all. He was Armenian. His Italian name came from a formal name change when he had been posted to Italy decades earlier. The chances therefore that he was a paid-up member of La Cosa Nostra or another Italian criminal organization quickly plunged.

No reports of any involvement in U.S. criminal activity surfaced, yet the Armenian link interested us because it had obviously been nearly completely hidden from view. A news search did not link us to anything negative about our man and Armenia, but we wondered if one of his companies could have been involved in Armenia—perhaps a company we had not yet identified.

We ran a "bad word" search on Armenia, including a few people known as notorious gangsters there, one of whom had also run afoul of U.S. authorities. There in one of the articles was our man with his name misspelled. Based on the description of this man's businesses in Armenia and the United States, we knew the reference was to our subject.

In the article, our man Mr. A spoke glowingly of another businessman in Armenia who would, a few years after the article was published, be charged with several counts of bribery.

Our conclusion in the end was that Mr. A was not a gangster, although to do business in the rough-and-tumble world of Armenia just after the collapse of the Soviet Union, you would be naïve not to expect to rub up against a few unsavory characters.

You cannot prove a negative, so we could not say for certain that Mr. A was *not* affiliated with organized crime. Instead, we delivered a more complete portrait of a complex character with no major defects we could detect. Our client was able to make a much more informed decision about the partnership.

Answer to Problem 2

We were able to demonstrate to the client that a simple round of interviewing former employees well before discovery began would have added a lot to the efficiency of the discovery process.

Companies do not post organization charts on their websites, and only the most rudimentary ones appear in annual reports—when they appear at all. The best way to find out who did what at a company and in which department is to call people who no longer work there.

Doing it this way has several advantages:

1. You are getting information that is not usually written down for public consumption, thus obtaining it this way is just about the only possible method.

2. Seeking out former employees avoids violating the no-contact rule, which permits you to talk to some members of an opposing-party company, but not others (see Chapter 5 on ethics).

Before talking to any of the people who told us all about the computer systems, the names of the departments and other information that was crucial for our client, we made sure to ask whether they had signed confidentiality agreements before leaving the company. If so, we terminated the calls.

After about 15 hours of interviews, as opposed to hundreds of hours in fruitless discovery, we were able to provide a concise, organized list of the names of the company's computer systems and department heads.

Was the information as good as what was in the company's files? Or course not. Was the organization chart full of holes? Probably. But in the world of high-stakes litigation in which even modest-size companies have hundreds of thousands of pages of documents, it was deemed to be a success both because of the information obtained and the costs saved.

–Appendix II–
A Starter List of
Investigative Databases

The world of legal information is dominated by two major companies, Thomson Reuters and Reed Elsevier. They also control the largest databases for nonlegal information that tells us where people live, what they may own and where they may work. The biggest ones are:

- Accurint, a unit of Reed Elsevier's LexisNexis.

- Thomson's WestlawNext.

- TLO, a unit of credit scoring company TransUnion.

All three of these are governed by several federal statutes that protect information from being retrieved except for permissible uses such as debt collection, fraud prevention, litigation or locating witnesses.

In addition, we rely on the following:

- Factiva, owned by Dow Jones, retrieves news articles, as does LexisNexis.

- Bloomberg News, which is famous for its vast amounts of financial information and is also the largest business news wire service in the world. Its journalists often cover stories other wires and newspapers simply cannot afford to staff.

These databases can be expensive, and several require a minimum commitment to sign up. Compare those costs to the services on the

Internet advertising a complete nationwide background check for $39, and only two conclusions are possible: (a) these database companies are making triple-digit percentage profits or (b) what you get on the Internet for nearly free is garbage. Experience tells us that (b) is the right answer.

—Appendix III—
A Starter List of U.S.
Public Record Sources

All of the more than 3,000 counties in the United States differ in the way they keep records. While many offer a lot of information on their websites, others do not. A few barely have websites at all, except to tell you where to park your car when you go there in person to do a search.

Check brbpub.com as a jumping-off point to find the county you are interested in. If you do not know which county to look for, type the name of the city or town into Google followed by the state and the word county. Most of the time, you will find an answer right away. Then go to the site and find the county's website.

For asset searches and background checks on business figures, an indispensable stop is the EDGAR database of Securities and Exchange Commission filings. Beware the free EDGAR option. It will not deliver complete results, which is why a variety of databases charge for searching securities filings.

Many people contribute to political candidates in the United States and need to provide a home address or employer when they do so. Federal contributions are logged by the Federal Elections Commission at fec.gov. There are also state equivalents, which should not be overlooked.

If your subject has a nonprofit corporation, the nonprofit's tax return may be available online. Try Guidestar.com. Form 990 gives an overview of top officers and the organization's expenses, income and beneficiaries.

–APPENDIX IV–
ASSET SEARCH CLIENT QUESTIONNAIRE

It is common for clients who are just starting an asset search to be uncertain about what information may be pertinent to an investigation. Below is a nonexhaustive list of questions that may help prompt a client to recall information that could be relevant to an asset search. Bear in mind that additional questions may be necessary depending on the particular facts of the case.

The questions are about the person being searched, not the client being interviewed.

1. What are their full names?

    a. List any other names you know they have used. Single names? Other married names? Variations of their current names? Have they used their middle name or initials instead of their first name, for example?

    b. What about nicknames? Sometimes people named Robert Johnson can be known as "Steve" because of a middle name or for some other reason (they looked like a certain Steve in high school, for example).

2. When were they born?

3. Where were they born?

4. Are they married?

   a. What is their spouse's name?

   b. Have they been married previously? If so, what were their prior spouses' names?

5. What are the names of their parents and siblings? Are they particularly close to parents and siblings, and if so, which ones?

6. Where do they live?

   a. What are the addresses?

   b. Do they own property there? Keep in mind this includes real estate, as well as cars, boats, planes, etc. And real estate is more than just homes: It also includes land and commercial buildings.

7. What phone numbers are associated with them?

   a. Home

   b. Office

   c. Mobiles

   d. Any phone number they used to have but no longer have.

8. Where do they go on vacation? How frequently?

   a. Do they own property there?

   b. What are the addresses?

   c. What are the phone numbers for those properties?

9. Where do they bank? Please list personal and business banking relationships.

   a. Currently

   b. Previously

10. Do they have investments?

    a. Stock? Bonds? Property? Other businesses?

    b. Do they have any paid insurance policies with cash value?

    c. Do they have any annuities that you know of?

    d. Do they have any retirement accounts?

11. Where do they currently work?

    a. What is the address there?

    b. What is their position?

12. Do they have any ownership interest where they work?

13. Do they or have they had any partners?

    a. What are the full names of the partners?

    b. Where do they live?

    c. What are their addresses?

14. Have they had any previous jobs?

    a. What were the addresses and phone numbers there?

    b. What was their position?

15. Have they had any ownership interest where they previously worked?

16. Do they currently own any companies?

    a. What are the names of the companies?

    b. What do they do?

    c. What are their addresses?

    d. What phone numbers are associated with them?

17. Have they previously owned any companies?

    a. If so, what were the companies called?

b. Are there any naming conventions they've relied on? For example, initials of names? City names? Variations on the same name? (St. Mark Co., St. Mark Associates, St. Mark Partnerships. Or consecutive names like Alpha I, Alpha II, etc.)

c. What did the companies do?

d. What are/were their addresses?

e. What phone numbers are/were associated with them?

18. If you were this person, where would you think the smartest place to hide assets would be?

19. Where would this person expect *you* to look for assets?

20. Look back over all of your answers. Is there anything about this person that's missing that could possibly help us find assets?

Permissions

The author gratefully thanks the Philadelphia Museum of Art for use of the photograph on the cover, from its A.E. Gallatin Collection as well as Leonard Lauder, donor of the great Cubist paintings reproduced in this book with his permission.

Attention law schools, colleges, corporations: Quantity discounts are available on bulk purchases of this book for educational training purposes or fund raising. For information contact Ignaz Press, P.O. Box 2897, Grand Central Station, New York, NY 10163 or sales@ignazpress.com

Acknowledgments

Many people helped to form my thoughts about investigation, but none more than my teacher of evidence, colleague and friend at the Benjamin N. Cardozo School of Law, the late Professor Peter Tillers. A renowned evidence scholar, Tillers rejected the teaching of the subject as a laundry list of items linked to the Federal Rules of Evidence. In his class, evidence was a series of puzzles. He wanted students to think for themselves about problems of gathering proof, and what the word "proof" really meant. Those who wanted spoon-fed instruction hated it, but I liked it so much that after graduation I jumped at the chance to help out with the Tillers course in Fact Investigation. If I have misrepresented any of his thoughts in this book, the error is all mine.

NOTES

1 "Wigmore's mammoth treatise on the law of evidence devoted little attention to the pre-trial process; as its title suggests, its focus was on the legal rules governing the admissibility and presentation of evidence at trial. The focus of Wigmore's contemporaries and successors was much the same; scholars such as Edmund Morgan, Charles McCormick and John Maguire talked about the trial, and little if at all about evidentiary processes before trial." From Peter Tillers & David Schum, "A Theory of Preliminary Fact Investigation," UC Davis Law Review, Vol. 24, p. 931, 1991. See also Peter Tillers, "Taking Inference Seriously: Upon Reception of American Association of Law Schools' Wigmore Lifetime Achievement Award, January 2015, at http://tillerstillers.blogspot.com/2015/01/taking-inference-seriously.html.

2 Arthur Conan Doyle, *The Sign of the Four,* Chapter 1.

3 Eric Kandel, "The Cubist Challenge to the Beholder's Share," in *Cubism, The Leonard A. Lauder Collection,* Metropolitan Museum of Art, 2014. Freud was a path breaker in his field, but the idea that we should not rely solely on what we see to perceive and record reality was hardly new. Renaissance art "abandoned the medieval way of representing reality, by means of experiential conceptions, and began to rely instead on visual perception, one-point perspective and natural light ... now Cubism involved a return to the earlier conceptual principle." Douglas Cooper, *The Cubist Epoch,* E. P. Dutton, 1976.

4   Emily Braun, "Juan Gris's Cubist Mysteries," ibid.

5   Braun, ibid.

6   "The Birth of Cubism" in *Cubism*, ibid, p. 26.

7   Cooper, supra note 3.

8   The list of long-unverified degrees that turn out not to exist is long, encompassing executives at Yahoo!, RadioShack and an admissions dean at the Massachusetts Institute of Technology, to name just a few.

9   John Berger, *About Looking,* Vintage International, 1980.

10   "You Know My Method" by Thomas A. Sebeok and Jean Umiker-Sebeok, in *The Sign of Three,* Edited by Umberto Eco and Thomas A. Sebeok, Indiana University Press, 1983.

11   John R. Josephson, "On the Proof Dynamics of Inference to the Best Explanation," Cardozo Law Review, Vol. 22 Nos. 5-6, 2001, p. 1623 (2001).

12   Collected Papers of Charles Sanders Peirce, edited by C. Hartshorne, P. Weiss and A. Burks, 1931–1958, Cambridge MA: Harvard University Press, (5.172), cited in *Stanford Encyclopaedia of Philosophy,* http://plato.stanford.edu/entries/abduction/#AbdGenIde.

13   Peirce, Collected Papers (5:171), ibid.

14   Nicely discussed in "You Know My Method" by Thomas A. Sebeok and Jean Umiker-Sebeok, ibid. See also in the same publication, "Sherlock Holmes, Applied Social Psychologist," by Marcello Truzzi: "The simple fact is that the vast majority of Holmes's inferences just do not stand up to logical examination. He concludes correctly simply because the author of the stories allows it so."

15   Tillers and Schum, "A Theory of Preliminary Fact Investigation." http://tillers.net/fpaper.html.

16   Pattern Criminal Jury Instructions, 1987. Federal Judicial Center, available at http://federalevidence.com/pdf/JuryInst/FJC_Crim_1987.pdf.

17   Umberto Eco, "Horns, Hooves, Insteps: Some Hypotheses on Three Types of Abduction, " in *The Sign of Three,* supra note 10.

18   Stanford Encyclopedia of Philosophy, http://plato.stanford.edu/entries/abduction/. But see also David A. Schum, "Species of Abductive Reasoning in Fact Investigation in Law," Cardozo Law Review, Vol 22, Nos. 5-6, 2001, 1645—1681, 1672: "Abduction generates hypotheses, induction tests them. These processes are often mixed together."

19   Viktor Mayer-Schönberger and Kenneth Cukier *Big Data*, Mariner Books, 2013, especially Chapters 2 and 3.

20   Joseph Jastrow, Duck-Rabbit Illusion, 1899. From Joseph Jastrow, "The Mind's Eye," *Popular Science Monthly 54* (January 1899).

21   Samuel Arbesman, *The Half-Life of Facts,* Penguin, 2012, p. 178.

22   John Searle: "Watson Doesn't Know it Won on 'Jeopardy!'" Wall Street Journal, February 23, 2011.

23   Arbesman, supra note 21, chapter on "Hidden Knowledge."

24   Most states follow the American Bar Association's Model Rule of Professional Conduct in this area: Rule 5.3(c)(1): "A lawyer shall be responsible for conduct of such a person that would be a violation of the Rules of Professional Conduct if engaged in by a lawyer if the lawyer orders or, with the knowledge of the specific conduct, ratifies the conduct involved.
      Model Rule 8.4(a) is also relevant: "It is professional misconduct for a lawyer to violate or attempt to violate the Rules of Professional Conduct,

knowingly assist or induce another to do so, or do so through the acts of another."

25   155 Cal.App.4th 736 (2007).

26   Lawlor v. North American Corporation of Illinois, 2012 IL 112530, (Supreme Court of Illinois).

27   U. S. v. Christensen, No. 08-50531 (9th Cir. 2015).

28   15 U.S. Code § 6801.

29   Health Insurance Portability and Accountability Act, 42 USC § 201 et seq. Knowing violations can carry a prison term of more than 20 years.

30   18 USC 1039. Violators may be imprisoned for as many as 10 years.

31   New York Penal Law Section 190.25- Criminal Impersonation in the Second Degree.

32   New York Penal Law Section 190.26- Criminal Impersonation in the First Degree; similar statutes exist in every state.

33   ABA Model Rule of Professional Responsibility 4.1 covers truthfulness in statements to others. Rule 8.4(c) says that it is professional misconduct for a lawyer to engage in conduct involving dishonesty, fraud, deceit or misrepresentation.

34   The New York County Lawyers' Association said dissemblance was distinguished "from dishonesty, fraud, misrepresentation, and deceit by the degree and purpose of dissemblance," and that "dissemblance ends where misrepresentations or uncorrected false impressions rise to the level of fraud or perjury. NYCLA Formal Opinion No. 737, May 2007.

35   See for instance Gidatex, S.R.L. v. Campaniello Imports, Ltd. [1999 WL 731609 (SDNY 9/20/1999], in which investigators posing as customers for

furniture were found to be operating ethically in asking low-level employees the kinds of questions any customer might ask. However, this court distinguished this practice from customers speaking to high-level officers of the opposing-party company who might have been covered under the no-contact rule (see below). In contrast, see *In re* Ositis, 40 P.3d 500 (Or. 2002), a disciplinary proceeding which imposed a public reprimand on an attorney who employed an investigator to pose as a journalist in order to get information from the lawyer's adversary. Luckily for the lawyer, the Oregon Supreme Court did not uphold the Oregon State Bar's 30-day suspension of the lawyer's license.

36 *In re* Hurley, No. 2007AP478-D (Wis. Feb. 11, 2009). The Supreme Court of Wisconsin declined to discipline a lawyer involved in deceptive conduct aimed at obtaining exculpatory evidence for a defendant facing child pornography charges. The lawyer had lied in order to gain access to the computer of a witness that he suspected (correctly) would contain the exculpatory evidence. Note that the opinion defines the permitted lying as "dissemblance."

37 Philadelphia Bar Association, Professional Guidance Committee, Opinion 2009-02 (March 2009).

38 New York City Bar Association, Formal Opinion 2010-2: "An attorney or her agent may use her real name and profile to send a 'friend request' to obtain information from an unrepresented person's social networking website without also disclosing the reasons for making the request. While there are ethical boundaries to such 'friending,' in our view they are not crossed when an attorney or investigator uses only truthful information to obtain access to a website, subject to compliance with all other ethical requirements."

39 See for instance Midwest Motor Sports Inc. v. Arctic Cat Sales, Inc., 347 F.3d 693, (8th Cir. 2003).

40 ABA Model Rule 4.2, comment 7: "In the case of a represented organization, this Rule prohibits communications with a constituent of the organization

who supervises, directs or regularly consults with the organization's lawyer concerning the matter or has authority to obligate the organization with respect to the matter or whose act or omission in connection with the matter may be imputed to the organization for purposes of civil or criminal liability."

41   The Telecommunications Act of 1996 (amending the Communication Act of 1934) Section 222 imposes a duty on cellphone carriers to keep customer information confidential. The Telephone Records and Privacy Protection Act of 2006 specifically applies to cellphone location information.

42   132 S.Ct. 945 (2012).

43   2013 WL 3213347 (June 27, 2013).

44   New York Penal Law S. 120.45.

Index

Notes are indicated by n following the page number.

A

Abductive reasoning
    deduction compared, 30–31
    example of, 32–33
    induction compared, 38
    meta-abduction, 35–38
    retroduction compared, 34
    risks of, 34–35
Accounting, 23–24
Accurint, 89
Agency, 68–69, 78–79, 103n24
Arbesman, Samuel, 52, 62
Archaeology, 22–23
Aspirations, 20
Assertions, repeated, 20–22, 42
Asset searches, 41–42, 54–58, 93–96
Assumptions, 20–21, 52–53. *See also* Abductive reasoning

ORDER FORM

Send this form and a check payable to Ignaz Press LLC to:
Ignaz Press LLC
P.O. Box 2897
Grand Central Station
New York, NY 10163

— — — — — — — — — — — — —

_____ copies @ $22.95 *The Art of Fact Investigation* 978-0-9969079-0-3 _____

Add $5.00 shipping for first book
and $2.00 for each additional book _____

Subtotal (Books and shipping) _____

Tax (NY residents add 8.875% tax) _____

TOTAL ENCLOSED _____

Check must be in U.S. dollars and drawn on a U.S. bank.
For online orders go to www.ignazpress.com

Name _____

Organization _____

Address _____

_____

City/State _____

Zip _____ Country _____

Phone_____ Email _____

For more information call (646) 861-8382
or email sales@ignazpress.com